REFLECTIONS OF A CLYDE-BUILT MAN

REFLECTIONS OF A
CLYDE-BUILT MAN

JIMMY REID

Compiled by RUTH WISHART

A CONDOR BOOK
SOUVENIR PRESS (E&A) LTD

First published 1976 by
Souvenir Press (Educational & Academic) Ltd,
43 Great Russell Street, London WC1B 3PA
and simultaneously in Canada by
Methuen Publications,
Agincourt, Ontario

Reprinted January 1977

ISBN 0 285 64824 1 casebound
ISBN 0 285 64825 x paperback

Printed in Great Britain by
Fletcher & Son Ltd, Norwich

CONTENTS

My thanks to Ruth Wishart for helping compile the material, for typing the manuscript, for encouraging and cajoling in turn. Thanks also to Rod for his forbearance.

J. R.

PREFACE

It was 1957 and I was twenty-four years old. I sat in the Glasgow to London train on the first leg of a journey to a World Peace Congress in Ceylon.

An attendant appeared with lunch tickets which seemed marginally better value than the pre-packed buffet car sandwiches.

In the dining car I found myself the only one in the second-class section. So I was ushered into the first-class car, presumably to save unnecessary effort. In the seat opposite was a gentleman, at least in the sartorial sense.

Dark jacket, pinstriped trousers, white shirt and grey tie. Exactly the correct amount of shirt cuff was on view. As the main course was being served he suggested I join him in a bottle of wine.

The ice thus broken, he confided that he had just brought off a highly successful deal for his company. He left no doubt that the company was indeed his.

I told him my destination. He was enthusiastic. He hated war, he was for peace.

I began to warm to him. Why did he hate war, I wondered. He told me this story...

During the last war he was senior officer in a section of allied forces advancing through France.

On the way they liberated a small French town. They were welcomed as heroes and liberators.

Comfortably ensconced in some civil building they used as headquarters, he recounted how he revelled in the hospitality and affection of the local inhabitants. Until the day dawned when the citizens returned who had survived internment in

Nazi concentration camps. The whole town turned out to welcome them, and the senior Allied officer had pride of place in the official reception party.

They looked, he said, 'like walking corpses' when they arrived. The Frenchmen hugged them and kissed them, bubbling like children.

'It was clear I would have to do the same.'

He did his duty, and rushed back to his quarters as soon as decency permitted for a bath and a change of clothes. The recollection was clearly loathsome.

When he finished I looked at him again. His features were refined, even sensitive.

Public school, a good university, a detached house probably somewhere in the stockbroker belt.

Doubtless well liked in his clubs, a regular attender at the local Anglican church and, in the conformist sense, a good husband and father. A good chap.

Yet in his description of this wartime episode there was not even a glimmer of sympathy or plain human compassion.

No feeling for people who had lived through the daily hell of concentration camp life.

His sole concern was with his own personal well-being and hygiene.

In essence he was not really so civilised.

As he spoke on, I thought of my friends and colleagues in the working-class and socialist movement. Of the miners, the engineers, the shipyard workers.

They could not be called refined. Most of them had never worn cuff links. I remembered seeing some of them at formal dinners looking baffled by the array of cutlery before them. But if they had been in France on that day they would have been crying alongside 'the Frenchies'.

I love them, and to them I dedicate this book.

AUTOBIOGRAPHICAL SKETCH

Leo and Isabella Reid had seven children. Three of them died in infancy. I can remember only Sally, of the three dead sisters, and she only vaguely. For she had been the only one younger than I.

Sometimes I used to ask where she was, why she wasn't there. But my mother would cry, so I stopped asking.

When Sally died I was left the youngest of two boys and two girls. I had been born in 1932, in the depression. Born in Whitefield Road, Govan, Glasgow, a slum clearance house.

It was hardly luxurious. The cheapest of linoleum was a luxury. My father would be out of work more often than not. My mother would send us to the butchers for a ham bone for soup, or broken biscuits and bread from the bakery. They were all weapons in the endless battle for survival. All part of the amazing ingenuity shown by the working-class mother in trying to nourish her family.

Yet within these limits I had a pampered childhood. Perhaps because I was the youngest survivor, my mother watched me with a concern which was almost claustrophobic.

The slightest cold was impending pneumonia, a sort throat meant the threat of diphtheria. Playing with children who had a history of tuberculosis was forbidden, for it was a killer.

My father tried to earn casual money from the docks. But the men with badges always got first choice. The badges passed down from father to son.

Some memories of childhood are very vivid. Memories of the time I went out to find work as a child, wearing my father's jacket trailing at my knees.

Memories of my mother standing at the window watching for my father, knowing if he came early it meant no extra cash.

The community at large was poor. Materially very poor. Yet my recollections are not unhappy ones, rather of people and families rich in character.

There were the Hopes, the sons all good footballers. One of them they called the sparrow ... perhaps because of the way he flew up the wing.

I met him again in Blackpool in 1975, unrecognisable almost as a happy portly man on holiday with his wife and family.

And the Garrity family, a family of boys and only one girl. Old man Garrity was a large forbidding sort of man, very proud of his pet canary. But there was also a cat in the household. One night Garrity came home and the cage was empty. The cat was on the hearth looking entirely satisfied with life. Old Garrity strangled the cat in a rage and threw it in the bin. Then he went to the pantry to find something to eat and the canary flew out.

And the Melvins. The mother I called Mecca and she was also my godmother. On hundreds of occasions when I was the imagined victim of some terrible injustice at the hands of my mother, I'd pack a little case with treasured possessions, and leave home to live with Mecca in the next tenement. Replenished and soothed by her tea and scones I'd be home in time for dinner.

At one stage they took me off to hospital with what they mistakenly thought was diphtheria. The ward was quarantined and some of the children were so ill they couldn't eat. I ate my own meals and theirs too. They sent me home after four weeks.

I investigated the house when I got back. Four weeks is a long time for a child. Then I ran round to see Mecca but only the girls were there, weeping. I ran from room to room and they told me 'she's away'. Then I knew that like Sally she wouldn't be coming back.

It was the first time I realised the finality of death.

Life was enriched, and often made bearable, by the spirit of community.

I would never try to romanticise slums. They are an affront to human dignity.

Yet in the post-war years the politicians and planners committed a further crime when they demolished some of the slums. For they moved the people to huge dormitory housing schemes, with no attempt to preserve the community, or give it the facilities from which a new community could flourish.

Billy Connolly aptly describes them as 'deserts wi' windaes'.

In those days, Govan life was rough and tough but there was that all-important community. In the tenements where I was raised, it would just not be possible for an old pensioner to die and lie unnoticed for weeks.

The one divisive element was that scourge of Clydeside ... religious bigotry. The Billy and Dan mentality. We were Catholics yet I was never conscious of any religious influences. Some days, coming home from school, boys would stop and ask you 'Are ye a Billy or a Dan?' You did a quick calculation and hoped you guessed their religion right before answering. If you got it wrong you got battered for your trouble. Looking back now it seems more tribal than religious.

The backcloth was the depression. Few jobs. Most men looking vainly for work. If the person dispensing employment was Catholic, then Catholic jobless stood a better chance. And, of course, the reverse. Yet during and after the war, in periods of relatively full employment, that bigotry visibly diminished. Perhaps if Ulster had had full employment, and a sufficiency of housing for all, the present problem would have smaller dimensions.

By the time I reached young manhood our family had no association with any church as distinct from Christianity.

My father, I think, influenced me, and for the good. He wasn't perhaps a decisive man, but with hindsight, I see him as an intelligent one. And this realisation is a surprise, for he did many silly, self-destructive things. When he had money he drank too much. He was a gambler with the gambler's conviction that he would one day bankrupt the bookie. Yet he had a tremendous sense of humour, loved jokes.

And right into the last years of his life he retained an almost child-like enthusiasm for some new-found interest.

Once it was goldfish and a tank stocked with amazing paraphernalia. My mother thought the tank looked murky one day and put in fresh water from the cold tap. It was December. My father came home from work, saw the aquarium and said a number of unprintable things. All the fish were floating at the top.

He mounted a rescue operation, all the while continuing his verbal attack on my mother's mental capabilities. One by one he took them out, stroked them, and gave them drops of whisky from a matchstick, before putting them in properly heated water. To see him gently work with those big calloused fingers was really something. I don't know how he did it but he saved them all.

Bella, my mother, complained that he hadn't treated HER with such tenderness for years.

He never belonged to any political party until he joined the Communist Party years after I did so.

But when he spoke about politics, he spoke of the needs for workers to unite and fight for the common interest. He was a socialist with only the vaguest concept of what he meant by socialism. He was never active in a trade union sense, but when Labour won in 1945, he almost cried with joy. He saw it as end of unemployment. It was like Hogmanay all over again.

Poor dad. His hopes, and those of millions like him, were to be dashed by a government that betrayed their trust.

I was thirteen in 1945, and living in a house with few books. But somehow I became a voracious reader. The inspiration was not from school any more than it was from the domestic environment. I had passed my eleven-plus without dropping many marks, but for me secondary education was almost a complete waste of time.

My friend Freddy and I were put in an academic stream. Two years of Latin and French and one of Greek. All taught by rote.

The teachers were diabolical.

One of the language teachers was a positive sadist. He used the belt with a brutality worthy of a warder in Belsen. And I say this objectively, having escaped his attention in this direction.

One of the women teachers in retrospect was sexually neurotic. She would tell us repeatedly 'boys and girls don't touch yourself'. While we pondered how to wash but not to touch, she would repeat with further emphasis making it clear she referred to our private parts. 'Remember,' she said, 'HE is always watching.'

One boy was a compulsive doodler. His favourite doodle was a round cherubic face with slanted oriental eyes. One day he started with the eyes. She took the drawing from him turned it right round and looked at him with horror. 'You filthy-minded boy.'

She used one class period to warn of Communism. Communists, she explained, were only interested in raping nuns. I had never known any communists. But I did wonder what women communists were doing in a movement for which they were organically unsuited.

Now in my more mature years, I can view this teacher more charitably. She was clearly sick. But it's a reflection on our educational system that she should have been let loose on children.

I knew I would be leaving school at fourteen. It didn't occur to me, or anybody else for that matter, that I should stay on and perhaps try for a place at university. Of all the people who lived in our tenements I can't recall one who did go to university, though I suppose there must have been some.

So my senior secondary education did not inspire a love of literature, music or anything creative. Yet I was hooked on reading. After school there would be the obligatory game of street football, dinner and then I went into the bedroom I shared with my brother John and read for hours. Stevenson, Scott, Shaw, Dickens. My mother thought I was sickening for something.

Shaw was a considerable influence then. By fifteen I had read everything he had written. Even at twelve I had been aware of class injustice. My school mates knew I was socialist in outlook. But I had no theoretical understanding. In his brilliant prose Shaw gave me the first glimmerings of socialist theory.

When I did leave school my mother gave me ten shillings from my first wage. It was an enormous sum. I borrowed another sixpence from my eldest sister, Isa, and walked several miles to the nearest bookshop. I bought Tom Johnston's History of the Working Classes in Scotland. The next day I was reading it when my mother came into the room. I asked for money for ice cream. She wanted to know what I'd done with the money she'd given me already. I told her. 'I'm not giving you money to spend on things like that,' she said. Fortunately she changed her mind.

The book, while by no means the definitive history of the Scottish working class, made a sizeable impact on me. I was angry, outraged by the catalogue of crimes against the poor of my country. Here was the real history of my people, not the pap fed into us in school.

So I added to my reading list books on socialist theory. The Govan library became a home from home. And it also included a section on newspapers and periodicals. It was there I discovered *Forward*, the socialist weekly then edited by Emrys Hughes, son-in-law of Keir Hardie. In later years I was to get to know Hughes quite well. A wonderful old character, a genuine socialist and pacifist.

The *Daily Herald* and the *Daily Worker* I ordered from a local newsagent. I paid for them with money from my first job, delivery boy for Galbraith's the grocers.

It was the first time I'd ridden a bike, and it was miraculous that both I and the groceries survived the first fortnight. I knew it could only be a temporary job, for I loved football, and I couldn't see any future in a job where you worked Saturdays.

Improbably the Labour Exchange sent me off to a firm of Stockbrokers ... Kilpatrick and Robertson of Renfield Street,

Glasgow. The hours were attractive and they didn't include Saturdays. I took the job.

David Robertson, one of the partners, was also chairman of the Glasgow Stock Exchange. He became very friendly with me, and interested in my progress.

My left-wing views soon became known to him and others in the office. And far from arousing hostility, they greatly amused David Robertson. He liked to think he had a bit of a Bolshie on his staff. If I brought left-wing pamphlets to work he would ask to read them. Within a year I was responsible for the firm's business in the clearance house.

Once a month, so far as I recall, all the companies sent representatives to the clearance house, a large room in the Stock Exchange. All the other representatives were men in their forties and fifties, but the company was sending me to courses at the commercial college.

The lecturer there talked about much which I found uninteresting, but during one lecture he said: 'The Stock Exchange will last for as long as the present economic system.'

At which I retorted, 'Surely we are entitled to more job security than that.'

By now I was a member of the Labour League of Youth, and was studying socialist economics. I had had my first introduction to Marx through a book by Emile Burns.

During this period, a youth parliament was formed in Glasgow at the headquarters of the Iona Community. Each party in turn formed a government. In the Labour government the Prime Minister was Gregor McKenzie, now a junior minister in the Callaghan government.

I was made Chancellor of the Exchequer at fifteen years of age. Some others were in their thirties, most were in their twenties. A few on the Tory benches looked to me as if they might be in their forties.

I was asked to draw up a budget in line with Labour policies. I took as my text the 1945 election manifesto 'Let Us Face the Future', and not the current policies of the government with which I had become quite disenchanted.

In the event, nobody checked with me before I delivered the budget, which included all the demands of the left and evoked a jubilant response from the young left-wingers on the Labour benches, and the young Communists.

The Tories were angry and the reaction from my own colleagues was one of consternation. But they were stuck with my budget and with me. They could hardly oppose what was supposed to be their own policy.

A few months later I left the Labour League of Youth. I felt that the Labour Government was moving to the right, both in economic and foreign policies. I had also been soured by my own experience in the League.

At one of the last meetings I attended, the conversation had turned to political ambitions. The most popular perspective was to become a local councillor, then go for a safe Labour seat. An end to deprivation, the economic and cultural emancipation of working men and women never rated a mention. My bewilderment turned to anger. I gathered my papers and left the room. 'Are you going to the lavatory Jimmy,' someone called. 'No,' I muttered. 'I'm leaving it.'

Till then the Labour Party had always seemed to me – both by upbringing and tradition – the party within which my own desire for a better Britain would best find expression.

But I had begun to feel an outsider. Politics wasn't after all a career. It was a mission, a dedication. Careerism was a poison that would finally corrupt the body politic of the Labour Movement.

I still hold that opinion.

Had I then been in touch with some of the thousands of good socialists within the Labour Party I might never have left. But all I could see was the petty careerists and a government lurching rightwards.

Now I felt I must put my own house in order. Working for a stockbroker was incompatible with my personal convictions. So the following Monday I said as much to David Robertson. He was upset, and told me that in a few years I would have my own clients and share the commission in their business. It might develop into a partnership, he added.

The prospect, kindly meant, was appalling.

And when it became clear that I meant to leave there was no antipathy. My memories of this man are happy ones. Despite our philosophical differences – which were profound – I liked him personally.

As I wondered what to do next, my pursuit of knowledge went on unabated. In those days in Glasgow, secondhand books were sold from barrows in many streets. You could buy books for as little as sixpence and I took full advantage.

The Brontës (I still think that *Wuthering Heights* is the best English novel), Zola, Fielding, Gorky and all.

I delved into Douglas' theory of the credit system; and Jean-Paul Sartre's existentialism. But it was Marx, and in particular his economic analysis, that was beginning to make sense out of the turmoil of ideas and contradictions that threatened to engulf me.

I used to go to the Workers Open Forum in Renfrew Street, Glasgow. It was used by all sections of the left as their stomping ground. In the debates, contributions would be interspersed with references or quotes from Chaucer and Milton, from Omar Khayyam and Shakespeare. I hesitate to be disparaging, for they helped to widen my reading and my interests. But the object of the exercise often seemed to be to score debating points rather than reach understanding. They also seemed in many instances to be intellectual elitists with a thinly veiled contempt for the great mass of the working people. My life style, my background, made it impossible for me to accept this stance.

Despite my precocity in terms of politics and literature, I was not the usual stereotype of the youthful bookworm. For I loved football.

In the late forties the Edinburgh team, Hibernian, were emerging with the best forward line I had ever seen. Smith, Johnstone, Reilly, Turnbull and Ormond . . . When they came to the West of Scotland my friend and I made sure we were there.

Jazz was then my favourite music. I had played trumpet in a

brass band at school, and still played a bit. Louis Armstrong was my musical god, but at that time I became interested in the modern school – called be-bop – and the leading figures in it, Charlie Parker and Dizzie Gillespie.

I played table tennis too for a local team. And last, and by no means least at all, I knew that the lassies were the best opposite sex imaginable.

I had begun an engineering apprenticeship in the tool room of a firm called Scottish Precision Castings, based in Hillington. It was a small place ... the tool room, a foundry and a larger unit with a labour force of girls who ragged and dressed the castings. I wasn't yet sixteen and the only apprentice there. I used to dread going to the toilet which meant passing through where the girls worked. I'd heard stories of similar situations where the lassies had an initiation ceremony during which they de-bagged the apprentice and painted his genitals.

But one day the call of nature overcame my terror. I asked a journeyman to come with me, and I walked on his outside as a barrier. Halfway there he grabbed me and pushed me among the lassies.

Fortunately they were all wellbred working girls and my trousers remained intact. Instead I was kissed, cuddled, caressed and fondled ... a far from unpleasant experience.

In this factory the engineers were well organised and on my first day I found the AEU. The leading shop steward was a member of the Communist Party, as were other members of the work force.

But I couldn't find a member of the Labour Party there.

The Communists impressed me. At tea breaks and dinner time discussions would start, not always about politics, but often enough. My own criticisms of the Labour Government were echoed by these Communists, developed by them into a coherent pattern. But above all they were good citizens, and this was where the anti-communism I had been fed at school rebounded with a vengeance.

Marx's *Critique of Political Economy* had long ago made a profound impression on me. I felt that anyone who rejected his contribution to socialist thought – particularly in the economic field – was a fool. I was prepared to accept Marxism as an important element in the development of socialist consciousness, but still not prepared to accept its apparent practitioners, the Communists. For the image of Communism instilled in childhood persisted. I was suspicious.

Yet I had met my first communists now, they worked with me, they were human, and sociably listened to what the other had to say before replying, not stridently, but with reasoned argument.

Life is full of maybes.

Maybe, as I said, if I had met more genuine socialists in the Labour Party, there I would have remained. Maybe if my first encounter with communists had been with dogmatic, sectarian communists ... But these were my experiences, and when I attended the Junior Workers Committee of the AEU in Paisley, Ian Towell invited me to go to a meeting of the Govan Young Communist League.

I was sixteen when I formally joined the Young Communists, and I took some of my pals along with me. The local branch met in a grimy little hall with boarded up windows in Govan's Golspie Street.

The cold war had just begun in earnest and it wasn't an easy time to profess Communism.

Meanwhile the factory where I worked went into liquidation, and I found a job as an apprentice at Weirs, an engineering works on the south side of Glasgow.

At meal breaks we'd have discussions and some of the boys became interested in Socialism. Some of them started to read the *Daily Worker* which I brought with me.

In industry apprentices rarely get the sack, at least not unless they commit some heinous offence like raping the typist or assaulting the foreman with a blunt instrument.

Our foreman was called Sam : a portly florid faced chap who probably suffered from high blood pressure.

He would walk up the passage between machines, stopping to make some remark to his underlings, then walk on and pause to turn and view with one eye the impact of his inane 'witticism'. The crawlers would slap their thighs with a careful impersonation of hilarity. Satisfied, Sam would carry on.

One day he stopped at my machine, flung open the door of my adjacent cabinet, and picked out half a dozen bonus cards.

'These should be handed in after every job,' he said. 'You're fired.'

I knew, and he must have, that most of the lads had cards as well ... ten, twenty, even thirty of them lying in their cabinets.

It was blatant victimisation, and the shop stewards' convenor said so. Jock Sheriff was his name, and subsequently he became a fulltime union official.

The other stewards, many right-wing, agreed with his view. But they added a rider ... 'You'll not get the men to fight for a Communist.'

It was some months later that I was able to resume my apprenticeship in a factory called Daniel Varneys. The atmosphere there was totally different – a good workforce that wouldn't countenance victimisation or discrimination on any grounds. This brought home to me that the much maligned left – in industry at any rate – is the real custodian of liberal values and individual rights.

By this time my family had moved house to a council estate called Priesthill. I had become secretary of the local branch of the Young Communists.

Reading and studying ... not to pass any exams but to expand my knowledge and understanding ... had become an ingrained part of my nature.

I began to discover my Scottish heritage. What a reflection on our education system, that a young Scot must seek this out for himself! I read Lewis Grassic Gibbon's classic *The Scots Quair* and Jame's Barke's *Land of the Leal*. Then Robert Burns, through him Ferguson and forward to the twentieth-century school of Scots poets – the great McDiarmid, Goodsir Smith and others. I studied David Hume the philosopher, and Adam Smith the economist – whom Marx had held in high esteem.

I learned of our Scottish history of nationhood, and remember arguing with friends on the left of the Labour Party that the dropping of the demand for a Scottish Parliament from the party's programme could be disastrous.

We were told the factory was closing, and moving to Wishaw in Lanarkshire. The apprentices were given an option of going there or joining Bristol Polar Engines in Govan. Naturally we opted for the nearer Govan. The men had no choice. They could move to the factory in Wishaw or have their cards. All that I had been reading about was being substantiated in life. Faceless men taking decisions, without regard to the social implications for workers and their families. They were merely profit-fodder, to be used or discarded to advantage.

At Polar Engines I began my relationship with shipbuilding. For it was a marine engineering establishment and sometimes we went out on a repair or installation job to a ship in one of the yards.

Every one of the apprentices joined the union, and we set up an apprentices' committee. Wages were miserable. Thirty shillings a week for the first-year apprentice ... about what it would cost to kennel your dog for a week's holiday. Then in 1951 an agreement was signed giving us a paltry percentage rise. We were all pretty incensed and called a meeting in Govan for all apprentices. We also organised a demonstration for the next Saturday in Glasgow and marched carrying a coffin with an explanatory poster ... 'He tried to live on apprentice's wages.'

It gave a lead that many had been waiting for. Committee meetings now became mass meetings with every major Clydeside establishment represented. Some of the men called for immediate strike action; others, including myself, wanted to broaden our base beyond Clydeside first. We sent messengers to the East of Scotland and the North of England, and there was a half-day token strike.

Then an All-Britain Apprentices' Conference was convened in Glasgow, and a decision taken there that called for an additional offer or we would all stop work. Nor surprisingly, our ultimatum met with no response whatever.

So we arranged for a Clydeside walk-out and organised another march and meeting. When the appointed hour came the factories went on but the apprentices went out. The demonstration grew as we neared the meeting place, and when I got there it was clear that the great majority had responded.

The one large firm we were worried about was Weirs, but round the corner of George Square came another group ... headed by Weirs. And at the front was my old pal from schooldays, Freddie. Afterwards he told me what had happened. There had apparently been an awkward pause in Weirs when the hour to stop work arrived. But he had already decided that even if nobody else left, he would. Thus he stopped his machine, put on his jacket, put some personal belongings in the pocket and walked up the passageway. On his way down the stairs he became aware of a clattering behind him ... all the lads had followed.

The strike spread into England, and it's generally believed that about 40,000 apprentices joined.

In almost all the factories we had the support of adult workers, who wouldn't touch work done by blackleg apprentices. Gradually, in some factories, production ground to a halt. It was impressive to watch how the young men had organised in a responsible and disciplined manner. Each factory had a representative on the committee, who reported to factory meetings. A strike bulletin was brought out.

In all, the action lasted three and a half weeks and ended only when the employers said they would meet the unions with an offer.

We went back to work as we had left it ... united in the resolve that we would meet again to consider the acceptability of any offer.

In the event the money was acceptable, and represented a significant increase.

Two experiences from that time stand out still. During the strike the youth conference of the AEU was scheduled for

Eastbourne. With Dick Douglas ... later to be a Labour MP for Clackmannan ... I was elected a delegate.

The committee discussed whether I should go ... for it meant being away for three days at a vital time. But they decided I should, and should try to have a resolution of support passed. So Dick and I went down. For some reason he was disqualified from participating but could stay as an observer.

The chairman was the union president, Jack Tanner, doyen of the then right-wing establishment in the trades union movement. After his address, I attempted to move an emergency resolution. Tanner ruled it out of order as being unconstitutional. I asked for guidance and was told by him : 'I'm not here to instruct you on procedure.' A differently worded resolution met with the same fate.

When the tea break came, old Tommy Sillars, the Regional Officer for Scotland, drew me aside. He told me that while the conference couldn't support the strike, it could ask the National Committee to do so. Once more I submitted a resolution, one that Tanner had to accept. I moved it without notes, for our case was imprinted on my mind. As the debate went on it became clear that it would be carried. The only opposition from the floor was from traditional right-wing areas.

But then Tanner did something totally unexpected. He intervened at the end of the debate and attacked both the resolution and my speech moving it.

I got straight up after him. What had he done for apprentices, I asked. He must be beginning to believe his own press releases. Did he believe that employers could be moved by his rhetoric, and verbal persuasion? If so why had he not succeeded in raising our wages from the present miserable level? And so on.

He took the vote and there was a greater majority than any of us had expected. For a while the conference was in chaos with hands being shaken, and journalists running out to phone their story.

The headline in the *Daily Herald* ran ... 'President Tanner versus apprentice Reid'. Jack Tanner was reckoned to be one of the shrewdest operators at conference in his day, yet I knew as soon as he had opened his mouth he had made a tactical error. Still my concern was for the men and not his ego.

But he compounded his error later that night at a delegates' dinner. As the meal neared its end Tanner said: 'You're a bright lad, you could go places in the right company.' When I enquired how, he asked if I was interested in a career in the trade union movement, or in parliament. If so – 'we can help'.

'Are you trying to buy me off?' I asked. 'No,' he hissed, 'giving you sound advice.' For the rest of the evening there was an embarrassed silence.

The other episode which stands out was almost farcical. A victory march had been suggested at the end of the strike. A route was chosen, banners were painted and stewards appointed. The route we chose was to have included Argyle Street, but the police refused permission. It was of small concern to me, but others were outraged, thinking that it was their democratic right to march there if they so wished.

I felt we had won and that was what mattered, the last thing we needed was trouble with the law. Yet I didn't foresee the ludicrous situation that developed. As the march went down Virginia Street, mounted police suddenly appeared at the bottom sealing off the Argyle Street exit. As agreed, those of us who were out front did not challenge the police. We called for an about turn.

As there were thousands at our back, this took some time, and when we started, other marchers were going down a parallel street heading for Argyle Street. Fearing a fracas, a few of us pushed our way to the front. But when we got there it was again sealed off by mounted police.

I made it clear to the stewards that the march had ended, and that we should disperse and go home. To set an example a few of us started to leave. We walked along Argyle Street's pavements and were duly followed by others who had decided quite literally to follow our example.

To get them out of that street, we went down a side street, through St Enoch station, and out of its front entrance. There was a wall there, and it was decided I should get up on it and loudly advise everybody to disperse. As I finished, a black Maria swept into St Enoch Square and out leapt policemen to arrest me ... for causing an obstruction, it later transpired.

For the last hour I had been at my wits' end trying to prevent arrests and now I was one. As the sergeant put his hands on me a little lad, improbably called Karl Marx McCulloch, rushed forward to berate him. He was arrested too. Three more standing near by explained that I had been dispersing the crowd. They were arrested.

We were pushed into the police box in the square, and tempers were getting a little heated. I told them to keep quiet and act with dignity. As we finally got taken from the box, it became clear that word of our arrest had spread among those already going home. The square was full of apprentices causing a far greater obstruction than had ever happened prior to the arrival of the police.

The policemen with me insisted on taking me by the arm as if I was Legs Diamond.

Willie Martin, a workmate and now a trade union official in Australia, grabbed one of my hands as I passed and shouted 'Don't worry Jimmy, we'll get you out.'

The whole episode was becoming ridiculous. I could hear a woman shouting, 'Leave that boy alone, away and arrest some criminals.'

In the van I could hardly keep a straight face. Big policemen looking somehow simultaneously grim and triumphant, as if they had cornered a mafia mob, and four skinny lads, one dressed, for some reason now escaping me, as a footballer.

Sheer farce, but more was to come.

As none of us had been inside a police station before we were told what to do. First empty the pockets. Mine were bulging with political and left-wing pamphlets. The sergeant took them one by one, holding only a corner as if the contents might be contagious, and put them in a large envelope. 'Not a communist by any chance are you?' he boomed.

Next was young Karl.

'Full name and address.'

'Karl Marx McCulloch.'

'None of your lip, you. Your right name.'

'Karl Marx McCulloch.'

The sergeant, face now reddened, made a threatening gesture. Trying with difficulty to look serious, I explained that it was his real name, and that we were not thugs.

Though I wouldn't try to predetermine the political or other beliefs of my children by their name, I was happy at that moment that Jimmy and Anna McCulloch had chosen to do so.

Each of us was finally put in a cell. Mine had a bed made of stone about a foot from the ground. Surely these couldn't be for overnight prisoners? Or maybe they put down a palliasse and gave you sheets and blankets.

Shortly the wooden peep-hole on the door was pulled back, and I was asked who I was and where I worked.

The policeman said he used to work there too. Five minutes later he came back to tell me he'd phoned my firm and told them where I was. I asked him why.

'You never know, they might come down and bail you out.' With a hearty laugh he slammed the spy hole shut again.

Ted Willis never met these guys in Dock Green.

Wee Karl began singing the Red Flag and some others joined in.

A few weeks ago they were only concerned with getting a few bob more a week, now they were in prison singing. I came to the conclusion that the establishment was daft.

Finally the boys arrived with bail money and we were released. We could only have been in for two or three hours at most. But outside in the street there were hundreds cheering, some even crying. I was embarrassed. It was good to feel their comradeship, yet how could I do anything but laugh at the events of the last few hours?

I had only one real worry ... how would my mother react? But that was no problem. She was mad all right but not at me. The police were the villains of the piece, arresting respectable boys like her James when hoodlums were running amok all over the city.

A few weeks later the trial took place, and it, too, had moments of pure comedy. We were all fined one pound.

In 1952 I was elected National Chairman of the Young Communist League in Britain. Active in the trade union movement, I was also kept busy with meetings and rallies all over the country.

My main criticism of the YCL, was that it tended to be too inward-looking. By then the cold war was at its height, and I suppose it was natural for communists and those of the left to cling together for succour. For there was a witch-hunt atmosphere directed at those who spoke for socialist principles. Left-wing Labour MP's were expelled, and the TUC was dominated by right-wing bullies, who steamrollered things through with their block vote.

Yet it seemed pointless to me, to meet with the same people two or three times weekly and then go away with them again at weekends.

For if you all agree on fundamentals, you can only discuss refinements of your theory, and refinements of refinements, until the dialogue becomes so abstruse as to be in danger of losing touch with any semblance of reality. It happens in many walks of life, and theologians must be particularly vulnerable, as must academicians working within a certain discipline. It can happen, and has happened, with the left.

It was a real danger in the fifties, but I had no trouble avoiding the pitfall. We had in the factory one of the few YCL branches in the country, a focal point for most of the apprentices. Once a month we would go out on a Friday night, meeting in a pub for a few pints and then going on to Green's Playhouse.

I was also secretary of the Junior Workers' Council of the AEU and it met on a Thursday, making sure to end business by nine so that we might repair to the Locarno Ballroom. Thursday night was cheap night and the talent was great. Lads who had been involved in the apprentice strike kept in touch and sometimes twenty or thirty would meet and go on to a dance. These weren't gangs as such. In fact I can't remember even one occasion when anybody was involved in trouble of any kind.

And of course we quite literally went to the dogs. The White City track, the Albion and, less frequently, Shawfield. Through my father I knew quite a number of people who worked for bookmakers. I also knew that those who bet invariably wound up skint. You can always tell a punter, low at the heel and high on expectations.

I had no moral objection, however. To be among the people seemed more important than floating on a cloud in solemn conclave with the converted and incidentally boring the ass off each other.

The point is best illustrated by a YCL social and dance I attended.

During the evening I was asked to sing, and responded with a rendition of 'Frankie and Johnny' after the style of an early George Melly.

It was, for me, just a bit of a giggle.

Later, in conversation with a leading Young Communist, I enquired how work was progressing on a cultural programme we had initiated.

'You've a bloody cheek to talk about culture,' he told me. 'Singing decadent American trash when you're chairman of the League.'

The man concerned is still a close friend, and knows better now. The truth was that I was a regular attender at the Citizen's Theatre, a fairly regular attender at Scottish National Orchestra programmes and continued my abiding interest in jazz. I was still reading anything I could lay my hands on, with the exception of Soviet novels from the late forties and fifties which I found, frankly, unreadable.

A lighter incident from those days concerned my old school pal Freddie Shiach who was also in the YCL. His weekly job was to deliver copies of *Challenge* to the Cardonald area in

Glasgow. One week he refused. And confronted by a member he said he wasn't delivering because he disagreed with one of the articles that week.

The offending piece turned out to be the tale of a young Komsomol leader lying under a tree on a beautiful moonlit night with his equally beautiful girlfriend. Holding her hand he gently implored her ... to make sure that she exceeded the production target set by the local Soviets.

Freddie's view was clear cut. 'I'm no deliverin' that shit. I don't care what kind of system you've got. There is no way you're lying under a tree with a fine bit of stuff and start whispering about the agricultural production rate.'

He had a point.

In 1953 my apprenticeship was completed and I was called to serve Her Majesty.

I could have avoided conscription by going to sea as an engineer, but I couldn't do it. I really believed in a conscript army. A regular army of professionals has its dangers, as was demonstrated by France at the end of the Algerian war. But a conscript comes from a factory, a farm or an office, and there he returns. He is less likely to conform to the dictum ... 'theirs not to reason why, theirs but to do and die'.

So it couldn't be shirked. I was duly enrolled in the Royal Air Force in October 1953. I was to report to Cardington Camp near Bedford. And for reasons unconnected with the military the day remains clear in my mind, for it was the day of the great football international between Hungary and England.

I arrived at Bedford in the morning intending to report at the last possible minute before the 6 p.m. deadline. In the local pub I asked the manager if there was anywhere I could watch the match on TV and he promptly invited me to the flat upstairs. It was ninety minutes of magic, a new dimension in football. For the duration of the game I forgot the RAF, and when it was over my host and I relived every moment. Then panic, a scramble for a taxi and off to the base like the hammers.

Cardington was essentially the kitting-out base where I was

issued with a uniform and a dress cap that spun round when you touched it.

After three days, all the men who'd joined up with me had been sent to square-bashing camp. All except me. I was there for six weeks and in terms of a transit camp became something of a veteran.

I needed no explanation. The liberal illusions in this country as to the neutrality of the state machine breed complacency. Almost disdainfully the liberal democrat dismisses the probability of the existence of a British equivalent of the CIA. I say the probability, but assume the certainty.

Thus I spent six weeks in Cardington while the RAF decided what the hell to do with me. I was a socialist and, in their terms, ipso facto a subversive. Of course if you were a Soviet spy the most credible cover is hardly to be known as a 'Left'. Logically indeed, I would argue that there must be more foreign spies in the Tory party than all the rest put together.

I despise spies, of whatever nationality and regardless of the area of human activity. In reading the experiences of men like Malcolm Muggeridge and Compton Mackenzie who were conscripted into espionage in wartime, it becomes clear that the professional spy is a nutter. Whether they must be so in order to enter such an odious profession, or whether they become so in the process of living a daily lie, is almost irrelevant. Had I the names of all the world's spies I would print them, and a description and their cover, simultaneously in all major languages and expose the whole damn lot. In doing so, I feel an inestimable service to humanity would be rendered.

As for conscript Reid. He spent six weeks poking at litter with a sharp steel-pointed stick. The humour of the situation didn't escape me.

Most of the time I shared a billet with a regular corporal waiting for his discharge. Occasionally a fresh intake arrived and went out again in three days. The corporal couldn't have cared less. Waiting with mounting impatience for his demob, he vented his anger on the establishment and the officer classes with a venom which made me look a pale shade of pink.

I did have a few quid, in fact more than I'd ever had before. Meanwhile sisters, brother, parents and relatives were all sending more, knowing that servicemen were paid buttons for the first eighteen months. Monday to Friday all recruits were confined to barracks – no hardship if you were only there for three days, but in my case it became almost claustrophobic.

The corporal said he knew a way out by what sounded like an assault course. In fact it consisted of irregular deep trenches through which he swore he knew the way.

We usually went to a country pub with skittles and darts and all the fun of the fair. Getting there was not the problem ... coming back was a pantomime. How my saviour didn't break a leg I will never know, save to observe that the drunk man has the elasticity of india rubber.

In time I became a sort of camp dogsbody. But every experience expands the knowledge. Once I was detailed to clean out the ladies' toilets in the camp dance hall. Until then I felt sure that young men were much cruder than young ladies. Ah, the disillusionment of youth! The murals of the walls exaggerated enormously the male genitalia. I pondered whether this was the result of ignorance or wishful thinking.

The fateful day finally arrived when somebody had made A DECISION. I was to go to Bridgnorth for square-bashing, and a special train took us there. The embarkation scene was almost theatrical. Drill instructors with two stripes screeched instructions as men panicked and dropped packs. It was reminiscent of a second-rate English war film.

In our first parade the corporal rapped out in the traditional clipped style ... 'Anyone in this shower read music or play a musical instrument?'

I paused for a moment anticipating having to move the NAAFI piano, which on reflection might not have been such a bad chore if it removed you from the decibel count of the drill instructor. But it was a genuine enquiry, for if they established that you could read music and play the trumpet, you could become a member of the military band. It meant being excused much of the actual square-bashing. Two members of our band were really outstanding, a trombonist and a percussionist. I believe the trombonist left the RAF to join the BBC Dance Orchestra.

My favourite national service recollection is the current affairs lectures. They amounted really to crude attempts at brainwashing. And the first one I attended set the scene for what was to follow.

It was a cold December day and we had just finished a session of marching, counter-marching, left- and right-wheeling, marking time and the rest of the nonsense. We were all pretty sick of being bawled out by anything that moved and sported stripes.

Finally we were ushered into the lecture hall, where shortly a young man with a sandy-coloured pencil moustache bounded in and strode to the slightly elevated platform at the front. He indicated that rank didn't matter in this hall and that after the lecture he'd be happy to hear any opinions.

'Today we are going to discuss communism,' he began.

The lecture that followed was unsurpassed for pure comedy. The combined comic genius of Chaplin, Milligan and Sellars couldn't have bettered his performance ... made all the funnier by the seriousness of his delivery.

'There was this chappie called Marx. A cold, sour chappie.' Then there were 'other chappies' called Lenin and Trotsky, who believed both in continuous revolution and in the exporting of revolution. This was the cause of world strife.

He continued in a similar vein before asking us for our views. We were nearly all national servicemen, mostly ex-apprentices with experience in industry. Some had been on the apprentice strike.

I readily admit to having some initial qualms about having a go. Then I decided he'd asked for it, and anyway there was nothing much to lose.

It was too easy. I asked him for his sources, what he had read of Marx, Lenin and Stalin, what he could quote as justification for the conclusions he had reached.

I won't say he panicked. But he quickly searched his notes and found no comfort there.

It became clear that he had never been asked a question before. I quoted chapter and verse to show where Lenin differed from Trotsky on the question of building socialism and his ultimate rejection of the possibility of exporting revolution. A flood of hostile questions from the others followed, asking, if communism had been responsible for world strife, what had caused the world war? Everyone left the lecture in a great state of jubilation, and subsequent lectures became bright oases in a desert of square-bashing and military drudgery.

The officer would finish his lecture and all eyes would turn to me to lead what was virtually a united opposition. And it took no great knowledge or ability to dissect the outrageously right-wing analysis of world affairs. What made it all so unbelievable was the fact that they were supposedly trained for the job.

Frankly I was a rotten soldier. I made a half-hearted attempt at the spit and polish bit, but mostly while the others rubbed away at everything in sight, I would be on my bed reading.

But there is no justice in this world. One day we were lined up for inspection. The man next to me had been up half the night polishing his boots and got a dressing down for being slovenly, and being 'a disgrace to the Air Force'.

I waited my turn in some trepidation.

As he approached, a flicker of recognition passed over his face. 'Ah Reid,' he said. 'And how is the international situation today?' 'Grim,' I replied. He passed on.

Later I was sent to an engine mechanics course in Wales.

Two incidents from then still stick in my mind.

I automatically became a member of the band at what was probably the largest RAF station in the world. One day the whole complement was to parade on the huge square. The band led the march and took up its place near the march-past dais. The tune we played was 'Sussex by the Sea' and it seemed to go on for hours. I've never liked the song since.

My other memory is of an inspection where you laid on your bed – in the prescribed order – all your equipment. Mine was laid out with my customary lack of care. The inspection was being carried out by a sergeant. Now I am aware there are many good intelligent NCOs in the RAF. In fact the NCOs run the whole she-bang, not the officers. But some of them are nutters. Our sergeant belonged in this category. He stopped at my bed, took one look and exploded. I accepted the lack of aesthetics in my layout, but felt his reaction was excessive. At length I discovered the reason for his near apoplexy. The stripes on my pyjama jacket were not running concurrently with those on my pyjama trousers. Rather drily I remarked that I doubted the effectiveness of Her Majesty's air force was being undermined by my pyjamas.

I was right in it then. Thinking quickly how to extricate myself, I took the offensive. 'Sir?' I was serious. 'It just occurred to me that such meticulous attention to detail is important in such a highly technological arm of our fighting force. Inattention to detail in a crisis could have serious repercussions. That's what I meant, sir.' He fell for it.

After finishing training, we were all being posted to Malaya. But we were told that we could apply for a compassionate home posting. Men applied in droves. Expectant wives, ailing parents, all the forms of domestic crises that youthful imaginations could concoct.

I had no excuses. I remember vividly the afternoon when we were all sitting on the grass writing out the forms for embarkation leave. Suddenly a flight sergeant came hurtling round the corner on a cycle. 'Reid, AC1 Reid.' He pulled the uncompleted form from my hand and gave me another. 'You aren't going to Malaya – you're going to Shawbury, near Shrewsbury in Shropshire.'

I spent the remaining eighteen months of my national service there. Some of us had rooms to ourselves outside the main camp. I was again a member of the band. We played for a number of stations in the area, so it was virtually full-time. We had a jazz club on the camp.

Quite a number of the men were socialists, and left-wing in their outlook. We started classes on political economy and I was elected tutor. Maybe they didn't learn much but I certainly did. As a tutor you had to read twice as much as the students. You had to grapple with the complexities of socialist and Marxist economics to try and convey them without jargon. Ricardo, Adam Smith, even Keynes had to be studied.

We were all interested in music, particularly jazz. It was in Shrewsbury that I saw the Mick Mulligan band with George Melly. Melly was dressed in what appeared to be a hand-knitted suit. He seemed to me then, and still does, the Robert Newton of British jazz singers. He hams it gloriously.

During this period there was a strike in the London Docks. Everyone in the station was mustered on the parade ground. A long list of names was read out, those were confined to barracks and to be packed ready to leave within two hours for a destination near London. Everyone knew that it was to unload the ships in the strike-bound docks.

I was on the list. Indeed, only a skeleton staff was to remain. Naturally we had been discussing the strike. It was in all the papers, and I defended the dockers.

When we returned to the crew room there was naturally a bit of kidding. The Chiefie (our flight sergeant) came in, and I formally requested an interview with our Commanding Officer. Now the Chiefie was really a nice guy, and tried to dissuade me, for he knew the reason behind the request. But I insisted.

The interview went as follows: 'Well, Reid, what do you want to see me about?' 'Sir, my name is on the list of those who may have to go to London, and it is understood that the object of the exercise is to do the work of the dockers.' 'That is correct,' he said. 'Well sir, if I had known when I agreed to do my national service that I would be used in an industrial dispute in the capacity of a strike-breaker, then I would have been a conscientious objector.'

'Do you really think that we are going to allow those bastards to dictate to us?' he asked.

'Who are the "bastards" you're referring to. Who is "us"?' I asked.

'The dockers are the bastards, and by "us" I mean "us", the people, the nation.'

'Well sir, I don't think the dockers are bastards, and it's my opinion that the people who are really dictating to us are financiers, bankers and a tiny handful of men who control our political and economic life.'

He told me to sit down and then followed an hour-long discussion on the state of the country, indeed the world. When it was clearly nearing its end, I reminded him of the reason for my interview, and made it clear that under Queen's Regulations I might have to go, but that I intended raising it with my MP. Then came the amazing sequence.

'Reid, I do respect the depths of your feelings, and do appreciate that this is a matter of conscience. You also have courage.'

With that he picked up the phone, spoke to someone and said: 'Take LAC Reid off the list for London.' That done, he looked at me and said: 'Reid you won't believe this, but when you walked in the gates of this station, I had a file on you on my desk.' I hurriedly assured him that I did believe it.

'Have you any complaints as to how you have been treated?' I answered that I had no complaints. 'In fact you are highly respected by both the officers and the men,' he told me. 'Anytime you have a problem, domestic or otherwise, come and see me.'

When I left his office the men were surprised that I was not accompanied by MPs and heading for the guard room. All of them, including the NCOs, were genuinely relieved. SO WAS I.

There is a humorous ending to this episode. Some weeks later, a friend of mine in the YCL, Betty Steward, was having an engagement-cum-twenty-first birthday party. She was becoming engaged to another friend of mine, Monty Meth. Betty wrote asking if I could make it.

I replied, asking her to send a printed invitation. On receiving it, I asked to see our officer, and showing him the invitation I explained they were close friends and comrades and that I could leave the camp at 11 a.m. with a forty-eight-hour pass and this would enable me to catch the London–Glasgow train at Crewe. 'Aren't you cutting it a bit fine?' he asked. I agreed.

He picked up the phone and got through to a Vampire squadron. 'You have a few flying hours to put in?' he asked. There was obvious agreement at the other end. 'I want you to take an airman up to Turnhouse next Friday morning.'

The day came and I made my way over to the crew room of the Vampire squadron. I was wearing my civvies. The pilot was a sergeant. He told me that under regulations you had to travel in uniform on an RAF plane. He saw my disappointment at the delay and said, 'Let's try and fix something.' He grabbed a flying suit from a peg and flung it to me.

Minutes later we were flying northwards to Edinburgh. It took approximately half an hour. I can remember the beautiful view we got of the Forth Bridge as we banked to make our approach. It was then I also noted that my flying suit belonged to a Wing Commander.

On landing we were marshalled into the RAF section by two young crewmen. Pushing back the glass frame I jumped to the ground. The two airmen jumped to attention and gave me a smart salute. Reckoning it would take too long to explain, I said, 'At ease men.' I got out of the flying suit, pushed it into the cockpit and thanked the pilot.

As the plane taxied away, one of the airmen said 'Sir the Officers' Mess is over there.' I asked for the exit, explaining that I had to get to Glasgow. As I walked away, one said to the other 'That must be the youngest bloody Wing Commander in the RAF.'

On completing my national service, I returned to British Polar Engines to work. That was in October 1955. Before the end of the year, I was the Convenor of Shop Stewards. It was a craft-conscious factory, which meant that the labourers, the so-called unskilled workers, were not organised. They were also poorly paid. We got them all into the union and put in a claim for increased wages.

The case was simple. The tempo of work in the establishment was set by the bonus earners, the machine men. Other skilled workers, such as fitters whose work couldn't be precisely timed, were in receipt of bonus in lieu. Our contention was that the same principle should apply to the labourers.

The management said no. We then had a meeting of the men. Only two options were open to them. (1) Take it through procedure. This would almost certainly be fruitless, for if you won anything through procedure, it meant a precedent that had then to be applied throughout the engineering industry. The Employers' Federation would bar such a possibility. (2) Take strike action.

They decided to strike. Inside the factory the stewards made sure that nobody did the work of the strikers.

After six days the Managing Director sent for us and conceded the claim. Without saying it, he had a face-saving formula. The object of trade unions is to win justice for your members, not to rub someone's nose in the mire – including employers – so I readily accepted. We went through the process suggested and essentially secured increases in the region of 30/- per week, which was quite a significant sum in those days.

During this period we also negotiated with the management to provide Christmas dinners for some of the local old age pensioners, and the workers would levy themselves to provide hampers of food and bags of coal for them.

We approached the local OAP Association, and asked for names of impoverished pensioners. The Secretary, Mrs Clark, smiled at our naivety. She took us round some of her members. It was really shocking. Old folk who couldn't remember when they last had meat for a meal.

It was the usual Christmas dinner, turkey and all the trimmings. The Shop Stewards provided some alcoholic beverages. It developed into a party with the old folk singing, and two old guys doing a comic turn. At the end we gave them a large hamper of food for the festive period. We told them that later on, two bags of coal would be delivered to their households.

Most of them were in tears, so too were some of the shop stewards' representatives, including the convenor.

My feelings included a strong element of anger. It wasn't charity the aged required, but justice, so we organised a mass meeting of the workers, and organised another collection, this time to finance a campaign for higher old age pensions.

We organised meetings, and eventually convened a conference in the McLellan Galleries. We sent out circulars to every factory, trade union, church, tenants' associations, local authorities and any and every kind of community organisation. We had no idea what the response would be. When I arrived at the hall, there were queues at the door. The hall was packed. It was to prove the launching pad for one of the broadest united campaigns in the post-war history of Scotland. All trade unions, every church organisation, such as the British Legion, was affiliated.

The campaign was based on the organised Labour Movement, but the dimensions of the movement far exceeded the organisation of the working class. I was elected Secretary. The response was so great we hired an office from the Furniture Workers' trade union, and employed a full-time shorthand typist, called Frances. Franny would come down to the factory at the dinner break, with a pile of correspondence, and, while I ate my sandwiches, she would take down replies and clarify or modify our programme of activities.

We launched a petition and secured over 300,000 signatures. I was speaking at meetings all over Scotland. The platform usually included trade union leaders, clergymen, Provosts of towns, and burghs and MPs.

Reference was often made to the significance of a young trade unionist spearheading the fight for old folk. I never saw any great significance in this. Injustice is intolerable. The fight against injustice should recognise no barrier of age, creed or colour. To me it was the most natural thing in the world.

My two main points were firstly that you judged how civilised a society was, not by the affluence of the strong and the greedy, but by how it cared for the most defenceless sections of the community, the very young, the old, the physically or mentally handicapped. By this yard-stick our society was far from being civilised.

Secondly the whole question of old age pensions really concerned the aged of the poor. The rich looked after their own. Golden handshakes from companies. Family trusts ensured their material wellbeing. Workers were lucky to get a watch or a clock on retirement, and a pittance of a pension. It confirmed my belief that workers were looked upon as profit fodder. When you were too old for this purpose, then our society just didn't care. We, however, must care, or sacrifice our humanity.

The simple, compassionate appeal evoked a mass response. We decided to deliver the petition to Downing Street, and to hire a special train to London with delegates from all sections of the Scottish community. We had a full trainload and a civic send-off from the then Lord Provost of Glasgow, Andrew Hood.

It may have been a coincidence, but within months the Government announced an increase in the basic pension.

About this time I started serious courting.

We had met at a YCL dance before my national service. Since leaving the RAF I had been so busy. Trade union work, public meetings, the pensioners campaign.

I also had my own pals who were apprentices at the same time. Saturday night was our night. If I had no meeting in the afternoon, we went to a football match.

The evening was almost a ritual. We met in some hostelry in the centre of town. The discussion varied – football, jokes, politics, literature, even modern art.

There was no such thing as abstractions. Everything related – or we sought to relate it – to our lives, our experiences. It wasn't sombre. Sometimes it was hilarious.

Then on to the dancing. The object, quite simply, was to get a 'lumber'. If the girl lived within a reasonable distance of your own home – lovely. If not – you saw her to the last bus, which left from George Square. There you met up with most of your pals.

Consciously I was ensuring that my social life was not exclusively with Communists. This is not meant disparagingly, for some of the finest social occasions I have experienced were with friends in the Communist Party. However, there is always the danger that if you mix solely with like-minded people, you can unwittingly slip into the belief that everyone more or less thinks as you do. You start speaking a sort of political short-hand – an 'in' language that makes it difficult for you to communicate with other people. And what if you are collectively wrong? Who is going to correct you?

One evening, however, we decided to go to a *Daily Worker* dance in the St Andrews Halls in Glasgow – long since burnt down. There I met Joan again. I took her home, not to the last bus, but all the way to Clydebank. It cost me a fortune for a taxi home.

My Saturday nights with the lads slowly phased out. Within two years we were married. I have made mistakes in my life, and no doubt in the future I will err. After eighteen years of marriage, I can only say that this was the wisest decision of my life.

Looking back at that time, my life was really good. Real satisfaction in what I was doing. As a young journeyman, I had real spending money in my pocket for the first time in my life. My life style changed slightly. On Saturdays we went out with other couples, with my sisters and their husbands, or my brother John and his wife. Instead of the public bar, it was a lounge. Sometimes on to a restaurant for a meal. I started going to the movies again.

Poor Joan, she saw more cowboy films than any other girl in town. At that time, with a few exceptions like 'Twelve Angry Men' or 'On the Waterfront', films were sheer escapism, and for my money, westerns were the best of the genre. They were simple. For starters, you always knew the baddy. Either he

owned the saloon, wore a dark suit with a waistcoat and watch
chain, and employed all the muscle in town; or he owned the
biggest spread in the territory. In both cases he had territorial
ambitions on the lands of the homesteaders.

The goody, usually a stranger just passing through, got
involved in this minor peasants revolt and put his fast gun at
the disposal of the people. The baddies always got beat.

At that time I got the idea of organising monthly discussions
of shop stewards. Instead of using union halls which were
usually quite dismal in those days, I booked a room on a Friday
night in an hotel. The cost was covered by having a collection.

The agenda was as follows: a half-hour lecture by someone
on a selected topic; after half an hour waiters were then asked
to come in and take orders; questions for half-an hour; a break
for replenishing glasses; discussions and a brief reply from the
speaker. We left time to have one for the road and an informal
chat.

They proved a great success. Willie Gallagher, that outstanding pioneer of the Shop Stewards Movement, heard about
'big Jimmy's meetings' as they were called, and volunteered
himself as a lecturer. This was a dilemma. Willie was a brilliant
speaker and lecturer. He was also one of the best-read men I
have known. He also had a 'thing' about drink!

A total abstainer himself, he expected everyone – particularly on the Left – to share his abhorrence. In addition, once
Willie got into his stride, it was not unknown for him to
ignore timetables and chairmen.

This I knew from experience, having chaired public meetings with Willie before. We didn't want to sacrifice a formula
that had proven so successful. We all enjoyed the fact that
nobody went on too long, the comfort of the surroundings and
the opportunity of having a refreshment without anyone
getting drunk.

The position was explained to Willie. With reservations, he
accepted the format. I chaired the meetings, but on that night
it was with some trepidation. My fears were groundless. The
old man was magnificent. He stopped right on the half hour,

and the waiters came in to take orders. Willie was grumbling in my ear 'Is this necessary? Let's get on with the business.' I gently reminded him – 'Willie, you promised.'

Then came the half hour of questions. At a signal from the chair, someone pressed a bell and the waiters trooped in. Willie grumbled even louder, 'They had a drink only half an hour ago.' As the drinks were being served, I asked him 'Why are you so opposed to people having a drink?' 'Jimmy, my faither was a drunkard. He broke my mother's heart.'

I actually knew that from something he had written, but I wanted to engage him in conversation while the waiters went about their business. 'But you are going to the other extreme,' I suggested. 'Not at all,' he barked.

A thought occurred to me and I blurted it out. 'What if your father had been promiscuous, and in that way had broken your mother's heart. Would you be advocating celibacy?' He looked at me for some seconds – and then I saw his eyes were smiling.

The evening was a great success.

I love Scotland. That statement needs no embellishment. Dai Francis, General Secretary of the South Wales Miners for many years, and a truly delightful, warm-hearted character, once translated a Welsh poet to me as follows:

'If you don't love Wales, you can't love the world.'

I feel an affinity with all the peoples of the world. Not as a cosmopolitan nothing, but as a Scot. I assume that everyone feels the same about their own birthplace, their own country, the place where their roots are. I had never any desire to leave Scotland, even temporarily.

Then in 1958, a request from the Communist Party asked me to go to London, to work full-time as a national officer of the Young Communist League. The reasons as explained to me were manifold. This was a bolt from the blue. Joan was looking around to try to find a room and kitchen in Clydebank, so that we could get married. Working for the Communist Party full-time meant a substantial reduction in my wages, and as we hadn't a stick of furniture nor any money in the bank, it presented difficulties.

In addition, some of my close associates within and outside the CP were opposed, on the grounds that I was the best known and respected trade unionist of my age in Scotland, and that I could best make my contribution to the Left by building on that base.

Personally I had never thought of my own position or where I was going. A characteristic some people find irritating even to this day.

I accepted. It had been my contention that virtually a whole generation had been lost to the Socialist movement through the image created by the dominant right-wing careerist elements in the Labour Party, and to a much lesser degree by the sectarian non-visionary elements on the Left, including within the Communist Party. The YCL, of itself, wouldn't and couldn't change this situation. But perhaps, with the support of the party, we could make inroads into the problem, and, most optimistically, at least start the process of re-kindling interest and enthusiasm in young people for socialist ideas and for the Labour movement.

I went to London in the early spring of 1958. During my summer holidays Joan and I got married. It took us three years to get a place of our own, a maisonette in south-east London. We were fortunate in some respects, for during this period we had lodgings with wonderful people, first Idris and Dora Cox, then with Nora and Jim Jefferies.

Jim is now a Professor of Physics at Birkbeck College, London. Latterly we stayed with Colin Williams, one of nature's gentlemen. Colin at that time was Secretary of the British Youth Festival Committee. By training, he was an artist, and did a pencil drawing of Joan that my mother-in-law appropriated, and I have been trying to get ever since. Colin and I were members of the EC of the World Federation of Democratic Youth. I was also a member of its Bureau. I didn't mind occasionally attending the Bureau, for it met in Europe which meant you could fly in and out within a matter of three days at the most. I gave this up after a couple of meetings, for they would argue for hours over formulations in a document which always had a grandiose title, like *An Appeal to World Youth*. My own experience was that the world's youth were hardly waiting with bated breath for our pronouncements. So what the hell.

There was no chance of my getting involved in their Executive meetings. These were held in places like Djakarta, Santiago or Guinea. It meant being away for weeks, and I reckoned my work was in Britain.

So poor Colin had to go. He went to one meeting somewhere in Africa. While he was there, a pair of his trousers or flannels were stolen. He reported it to someone. Uproar ensued. For such a thing to happen to an honoured guest besmirched the name of the revolution. When and if the culprit was found he would be hanged! You have got to know Colin to realise his horror. He couldn't hurt a fly. He spent the remainder of his stay in an absolute hell, fearful lest his trousers be recovered.

In the latter part of 1958, I was elected National Secretary of the YCL. In fact I was the only full-time official working nationally. The funds were low, almost non-existent. The Party was operating on a shoe-string, and what assistance it could give was limited.

Joan was pregnant. The Party guaranteed my weekly wage, and without this, it would have been impossible for me to continue.

But things began to improve. There was a core of potentially outstanding young people in the League. To unleash their ability and energy in response to the problems and questions agitating the minds of young people, in a principled yet non-sectarian way, was surely the way to advance.

The campaign against nuclear weapons was beginning to stir the minds of youth. After some initial hesitancy, the YCL supported this movement. The reasons for hesitancy, on reflection, were interesting.

Firstly it was petty bourgeois. So What? Whose fault is it

that this was so? Our fault! The responsibility for bringing young workers into the struggle lay with the Left. The fight for peace required a movement that would struggle on all the issues concerned with preventing war. Fair enough. But the CND, as its title expressed, had selected one issue on which to campaign. What's wrong with that? Other organisations sought to fulfil the role in the general fight for peace.

If the cold war has receded, as I believe it has, a significant contribution to this was the scores of thousands of men and women – and particularly young people – who marched and demonstrated in Britain and in other countries, in the late fifties and sixties.

Once roused from lethargy, people start to question, to probe, seeking answers. In part, what happened was in response to the morally squalid mentality and myth of the 'You've never had it so good' era. In literature and drama, it expressed itself in the 'Angry Young Men' generation of intellectuals. In mass terms it was Aldermaston.

In totality their writings, songs and actions amounted to a mass critique and indictment of the capitalist establishment and its values. Of course they had no alternative, as some smart Alecs on the Left were quick to point out. No wonder, when socialism had become almost a dirty word in the higher echelons of the Labour movement.

They even wanted to delete Clause Four – the aim to socialise the means of production and exchange – from the Constitution of the Labour Party. The responsibility of presenting a credible socialist democratic alternative belonged to the Left.

In part this happened. But the complete task exceeded our capacity, and our resources. The YCL played its part during this period. We were able to employ more full-time workers. Gerry Pocock, John Delahey, John Leigh, Jimmy Whyte, Betty Meth, Pete Carter are names that spring to mind. The real strength lay in the areas and branches.

The cultural differences between students and young workers in general, started to diminish.

I remember my old friend Charlie Bruce, writing to say that his youngest son Jack, who had studied music and classical guitar, had come to London. He had given him my address and told him that if he was broke to contact me, that I would fix him up with shelter and give him money to get home, and that his father would recompense me. Of course I agreed. The next I heard, Jack was playing with Manfred Mann, and then was part of another group called The Cream which sold millions of albums.

I consider myself lucky and privileged to have been Secretary of the League during this period. We had problems, but the comradeship was real and genuine. I always spent New Year in Scotland. Even in these matters I am a devolutionist.

Joan usually went home earlier in December. One of the girls in the office, Hilda, helped Joan get to Euston. Hilda carried the bag as Joan's hands were occupied with the baby. Joan's purse either fell, or was stolen from the bag. I knew nothing about it until I returned from the office. Hilda was in tears, but before any explanations, Gerry Pocock handed me an envelope with money. The lads had taken a quick whip round and raised the full amount that was lost.

In 1959 I was elected to the NEC of the Communist Party and then to the Political Committee. On the PC were legendary figures in the Communist movement – Willie Gallagher, Peter Kerrigan, J. R. Campbell, R. Palme Dutt and Harry Pollitt.

Harry was an extraordinary man. From the outset, he made me welcome. To say he was charming sounds false, but his affection was real. At that time he was Chairman of the Party, and for health reasons his commitments were limited. Some evenings, if I was working he would invite me out for a pint. He had a fund of anecdotes. I could tell when he was kidding by looking at his twinkling eyes. Otherwise he could string you along with some tall stories.

Big Peter Kerrigan, who was particularly close to Harry always fell for it. Harry knew the British Labour Movement like the back of his hand and genuinely loved the working class. To speak to workers was a privilege, so was going to a meeting well dressed and groomed. I do believe that he had a certain distrust of anyone who hadn't a proletarian pedigree.

Maybe this had something to do with the fight in the twenties to prevent the party falling into the hands of what Harry would describe as 'bohemians'. He used to lecture Joan about looking after me. 'Mass leaders don't grow on trees as I well know.'

One night Joan and I were invited to a reception. We couldn't find a baby sitter. 'Bring her in here,' he said. 'I will baby sit.' So he did, and changed Eileen's nappy. When we returned he was crooning to the baby in her carry-cot.

The last meeting Harry spoke at in Britain was in Essex. It was Thursday night and I was the supporting speaker. The next day there was a little party at the office to wish him bon voyage. He was going to Australia to do a series of meetings. As he left the building, he stopped at the window in the entrance and shouted for me.

'That story you told last night to illustrate socialist morality, can I use it in Australia? I will give you full credit.'

That June I was on holiday at a caravan site on the Ayrshire coast. I had gone to the dairy for rolls and milk, pushing Eileen in her little pram. Joan was making the breakfast and listening to the radio. When I returned Joan, obviously shaken, met me at the door and said, 'It's just been on the radio. Harry has died in Australia.'

I walked down past the pier at the village called the 'Maidens' to some deserted sand dunes, flung myself down and wept.

My own opinion is that Harry never really recovered from the Twentieth Congress of the CPSU, and the revelations associated with Stalin's name. I am convinced that he and the other old British Communists didn't know. Whatever cynics may say, I am certain of this.

Similarly with the ETU – the political leadership of the Communist Party were totally unaware of what was going on. Indeed, before the trial, some of those involved were told to come to King Street. Harry asked them if there was any truth in these allegations of ballot rigging. They swore it was all lies and everything would come out at the trial. It did.

Everything in my life confirms the conviction that power and position is morally valueless, indeed corrupting, unless it's with the conscious assent and consent of the people.

Looking back at the leadership of the Party when I joined it as a comparative youngster, one thing stood out. The old guard, as the Press would describe them, were almost without exception products of the struggle of the British people. They were leaders, mass leaders in their own right. In my experience, they were not unresponsive, in the light of new information and knowledge, to new ideas or new concepts. But they could not implement them. Even if the will was there, age, and in some cases death, made sure of that.

In 1964 I left the Secretaryship, and returned to Scotland, where, after a short period, I was elected Secretary of the Scottish Committee of the CP.

We moved to Clydebank, where we were on the waiting list for a house. We stayed for a while with Joan's parents, John and Emily Swankie, before setting up house in the Faifley area. By then we had two daughters, Eileen and Shona.

The congress of the Scottish Party was to take place some months after my election as Secretary. It was decided that we should produce a resolution on Scotland, dealing with the Scottish economy including fisheries, forestry and agriculture. We should also re-state and clarify our position on the national question and call for the Scottish Labour Movement to lead the campaign for a Scottish Parliament.

We sent the resolution out to the Press, political parties, trade unions and other bodies asking for comments or criticisms.

Without knowing it at the time we made history. It was apparently the first time that the Press had been invited to a Congress of the Communist Party in Scotland.

It seems so incredible that I still think it must be wrong. The congress was quite successful. This was in some measure due to the painstaking research undertaken by an old colleague, Bob McElhone. The really significant point is that we made sure that the Left in the Scottish Trade Union Movement was aware of our analysis and argument on the National Question.

The STUC took a stance on the demand for a Scottish Parliament or Assembly years in advance of the Labour Party. One can only wonder now, what would have happened in the intervening years if the Labour Party in Scotland had paid a little more attention to a document sent to them twelve years ago.

I worked as Secretary of the Scottish party for nearly five years. Then, when our third daughter Julie was born, it became clear that the family income was totally inadequate even for essentials. Because of the age of the children Joan couldn't work, so we lived on the Party wage. I raised with the Party the question of leaving full-time work. John Gollan, then General Secretary, had a long discussion with me.

I respect and like the man. When you get to know him, break through his natural reserve, he is good company. It must always be in a smallish circle of friends, then if you start a subject he is interested in, like mountaineering, he's away. In larger gatherings he tends to be withdrawn, almost as if assailed by self-doubts in his ability.

For Johnny always underestimated his own ability, and also his standing and authority within the Party. I always found it difficult to say 'no' to Johnny. On this occasion I had to refuse his offer of a supplementary increase in my wage, to ease the financial problems of the family. This seemed to me to be quite unacceptable on the principle that if party wages were inadequate, they should be increased for everyone.

To be frank I was not unhappy to leave for a number of other reasons. While working as Secretary of the Party in Scotland, I was elected as a Councillor for the Seventh Ward in Clydebank. This was indicative of my approach to full-time work in the CP: leaders can't 'lead' from behind. You can't inspire or orientate others towards mass work among the people, if you yourself cannot work among them. And if the style of work prevents you from doing so, then change the style of work. Too much time was spent compiling statistics that informed us we were standing still. I bloody well knew that. So did anyone with eyes to see.

In other parts of the country it was worse. They had statistics showing they had gone back.

One of the problems was that full-time workers, particularly at area level, were being placed in impossible situations. They had to raise money to send into the Scottish office as their contribution to maintaining the party machine. This was sometimes at the expense of their own wages. This in turn meant raising more money to pay the next instalment, plus paying their arrears of wages, plus trying to ensure their current week's wages.

Desperate for short-term results, short cuts were attempted. By-pass the branches, try and do it yourself. Run harder and harder to stand still. It must have been heart-breaking. I saw one intelligent young man reduced to a near nervous wreck in six months by this sort of pressure.

We tried to change this. All full-time workers in Scotland were to be paid from the Scottish office. If there wasn't enough money we all suffered. If this continued then we had more workers than the party could sustain, so we would reduce the number of full-time workers. By and large it worked.

The other aspects were more difficult to change.

The pressure for immediate results came from the head office in London. On occasions, I told my colleagues to ignore them and proceed with what we were doing. Highly unorthodox to say the least. Ultimately I would have to carry the can. As things worked out, relatively speaking, we weren't doing so badly. We became quite substantially the biggest district in the country. Not through any dramatic advance, but by decline elsewhere. I think in 1969 we must have represented something approaching 25 per cent of the total membership in Great Britain. If you ask me was our membership organised in a network of functioning branches – the answer is no. It varied. Totally non-functioning to excellently organised active branches. The majority were in between, limping along.

Yet on an issue of great import, or through some public activity, the membership would respond. I once summed up my feelings to Alec Murray thus: 'To hell with the statisticians, give us the politicians.' I am afraid I just started ignoring anything that was not concerned about turning our attention to the public, public work, or the Labour Movement. The people are the arbiters of change. It was time to go.

I got a job at the Upper Clyde Shipbuilders, Govan Division, at my trade as a fitter. I was re-elected to the NEC and PC of the Party. I envisaged a period of what, for me, would be relative tranquillity: work as a Councillor, occasional meetings, University debates and being involved in what I considered a most interesting area of work – the dialogue with Christians.

After a period I was transferred to Clydebank, which suited me as it meant less distance to travel to work. A few months later I was elected AEU Convenor and the Chairman of the Outfit Trades.

By normal standards this level of involvement might appear hectic. To Joan and me it was a wonderful change. I bought an old Morris Minor for £40. It never broke down. Even on long trips with the family including the cat, to places like the Mull of Kintyre, it functioned impeccably. Maybe this model was too good, and that's why they have stopped producing it. Our neighbours by this time were all close friends.

Old friends, new friends. Old interests, new interests. All fusing together. Clydeside, the Glasgow conurbation, is often maligned. Rough, tough, unlovely are just some of the adjectives heard from fleeting visitors. But stay for a week or two. You can actually hear its big heart beat. Belsize Park will never seem the same again.

Take a car to the centre of Glasgow. Point it any direction and in half an hour you're in the country. Real countryside, with real grass, heather, hills, rivers, lochs and even mountains. Not landscaped grass carpets, on which you're frightened to stub out a cigarette lest you burn a hole.

This is the real thing and so are the people. Something that certain government ministers forgot when they decided to 'butcher' the shipyards on Upper Clyde.

It started with a phone call asking the leading shop stewards to meet Mr Ken Douglas, the managing director of UCS right away. None of us had an inkling of what was going on. Ken's opening words were, 'We are being forced into liquidation.'

So began the saga of the UCS. Another struggle. I was just thinking of buying some clubs and taking up golf. There goes the golf.

COMMUNISM

Based on a speech delivered to Dundee Communist Party, 1966.

> *Man's dearest possession is life. And since it is given to him to live but once, he must so live as to feel no torturing regrets for years without purpose; so live as not to be seared with the shame of a cowardly, trivial past; so live that dying, he can say: 'All my life and all my strength were given to the finest cause in the world – the liberation of mankind.'*
>
> Nikolai Ostrovsky

What is Communism?

The challenge of Communism is very much the outstanding feature of the twentieth century. Communism cannot be ignored even by its enemies. It is a world force, an ideological force, a political force on this planet, and it is also an international movement which has significantly contributed to all the social and political developments of the last fifty or sixty years.

Well over a hundred years ago, two young men in their twenties wrote a pamphlet for the IWA – the International Workers Association. It was called, *The Communist Manifesto.* 'There is a spectre haunting Europe, the spectre of Communism' – that is how they started this historic pamphlet. Since then, Communism has become a reality in terms of a political movement, unprecedented in human history. A movement that has had its set-backs and its achievements but which has, none the less, contributed to fundamental changes already this century, and is dedicated to changing the world for the better. As a philosophy, it has gripped the minds of millions. It has, I contend, helped man to understand the world. But in a revolutionary sense, not only should man understand the world, but understand how to change it, and that was the challenge thrown down by Marx to all other philosophers and philosophies.

Over this century, many people have spent almost a lifetime endeavouring to refute the philosophy of Marxism and Communism. In all the public libraries of Britain, there are shelves of books proclaiming that the authors have totally refuted Marxism. These authors are long since forgotten, while Marxism and Communism go from strength to strength.

What is this Communism that so frightens all the reactionaries, all privileged sections of the community and the all-powerful? Ideologically they laughed at it, sought to destroy it and failed. Some resorted to force using bullets to destroy it. This method has been tried by Hitler, Mussolini and Franco. Hitler and Mussolini are gone, General Franco has gone, yet Communism remains. All kinds of repressions have been attempted. One has only to mention the unlamented Senator Joe Macarthy of the USA with his witch-hunts, and the activities of the extreme right in Britain and elsewhere. They have failed. Communism seems to have this capacity to develop in people another incorruptibility, a dedication to the working class and the cause of Socialism, that cannot be intimidated nor bought.

Consider Willie Gallagher, who all his life served the working class, served the cause of Socialism and died as a tenant of a two-room-and-kitchen in a council house in Paisley. Compare his life with those of some of his contemporaries, who were also involved in the struggle on behalf of the working class of Clydeside in the early part of this century, and who ended up, regrettably, in the House of Lords, or living in the stockbroker belt in the south-east of England.

So what is this Communism? I think it is three component parts which are inter-related and inter-dependent.

First of all it is a philosophy. There are many aspects of this philosophy and I want to deal with only one here, which I think conveys at its best the majesty of ideas of Socialism and Communism. It concerns our understanding of history. What is the secret of history, how can we understand it? History is simply the story of man on this earth. There is a capitalist concept of history – and I'll be accused here of over-simplifying – which sees history as the story of outstanding individuals. It is the pedigree of kings and queens. It suggests to us that the people who really create history are swashbuckling 'Errol Flynn' characters who, with a successful thrust of a rapier, change the whole course of man's destiny. And it consigns the great mass of the people to a spectator role, to a role where, in historical terms, they contribute nothing to any progressive development in mankind's history.

But surely the intelligent approach is to look below the superficial, to try to discover the laws which govern the development and evolution of human society. There must be laws. There must be a basis for a scientific analysis of the development of human society. There must be laws governing our development, and when one looks there is a pattern to human history.

Whatever the difficulties, there has been a progressive onward march of man down through the ages. The ordinary people are still exploited today, but if you look at it historically, they've won greater freedom for themselves and for their class with each succeeding century. That the feudal peasant was exploited is undeniable, but his position was an advance on that of the slave in slave society. So too in capitalist societies – yes, the great majority of the working class are exploited, but we recognise that they have won advances and are in a much more progressive stage than the peasant under feudalism.

The tools with which man works upon nature determine the total wealth produced. And the distribution of that wealth is determined by the character of the society in which we live at any given moment. But the essence of human progress, particularly in terms of living standards, is determined by the development and improvement of those tools. A cave man's existence was determined fundamentally by the limitation of tools with which he worked to extract from nature the needs for human life. His tools were primitive in the extreme. We are better than the cave man, in terms of the provision of the basic needs of life, fundamentally because of the tools with which we work upon nature.

Over the centuries we have been tremendously transformed, indeed improved above all recognition. Consider for example, the highly mechanised pits extracting coal from the bowels of the earth and compare them with those of one hundred years ago.

For the secret of history, Communism says – it is one of the laws – is that a society which obstructs or prevents the development of the productive resources, is pressed into decline; while the society that enhances the development of productive resources is progressive, and, in historical terms, to that society belongs the future.

Now if you apply this law to the world today, Capitalism is torn with basic contradictions. For believers in economic and industrial activity as it is practised in Capitalist societies, the sole object of production is profit, private profit. Employers don't build a factory in order to create work. They build a factory to create profit – it is the sole criterion of their activity. How to maximise profit. And in maximising profit, you want to purchase the labour crucial to the productive process at the lowest possible price. And, on the other hand, to increase production per capita to the highest possible level.

Now there's a contradiction here. Working people constitute the great majority of the people, for they constitute the greatest percentage of the potential market. Hold down wages and earnings and you restrict the ability to purchase what you as a class have produced. So increasing the production of goods results inevitably in a situation where the people can't buy back the goods they produced. It is a crisis the Capitalist economists call over-production, but which is in essence a crisis of under-consumption. Yet their solution is to destroy productive resources.

The classic example was in the 1930s when Capitalism destroyed factory after factory, yard after yard. There were fishermen going out to sea, and coming back with trawlers full of fish. Because the people had no money to purchase the fish, they took the fish out to sea again and dumped it. In other words, they saw a glut of fish, in a context where the people were starving. That was in the 1930s. And even in the post-war years, in the United States we have had agricultural policies which bought so-called surplus wheat and potatoes for packing away in silos, until they were all unfit for human consumption: at a period when sections of the American people were under-nourished, and over the world as a whole literally hundreds of millions of people were dying of starvation.

Post-war, the face of Capitalism has changed, but the tendencies towards world crisis remain, resulting in arms drives for example. In the United States, when industry was running into difficulties, a convenient "crisis" has always emerged, and Congress demanded that the country spend more and more money on armaments. In a certain sense this too is destruction of productive capacity, by diversifying it into weapons of destruction, instead of using industrial tools for construction and re-construction.

In Britain, so all the economists tell us quite openly, the basic economic policies predominating ever since 1948 have been policies of 'stop-go'. But what does 'stop' mean? That you lay off productive capacity available to you. You stop production. You create unemployment. You do not utilise your productive capacity. You can examine whole branches of the British economy, and see the process at work. Steel for example, has never worked to its full capacity in the post-war years.

The situation is that the productive resources within society today have matured to the extent that we could easily be in the throes of a new industrial revolution, with all the attendant possibilities of creating an abundance. In a short space of time, we could virtually eliminate every pocket of deprivation in this country, if these forces were utilised.

Yet if you allow these things to remain in the kirk of an outmoded society and in the control of a class of people – the Capitalists – whose sole concern is profit and not the expansion of human horizons, then all our wonders of science and technology become prostituted. They become perverted and distorted and indeed in the last analysis cannot be used to the maximum for the people. In other words, they obstruct, they are standing in the way of the next stage of man's historical progress. They can't utilise the new productive resources and forces that are emerging.

And there is in many minds the prostitution of science. Nuclear power as related to the nuclear bomb. That's the view of electricity from the stand-point of the electric chair. Nuclear physics are neutral. Their perversion is a horror weapon of destruction. The responsibility for that belongs to society, and it is social and political factors that have corrupted what could be a blessing to man.

How can the development of productive resources proceed, in the set line of every Capitalist ruling class in the world today? They tell their workers 'in the national interest you've got to work harder, produce more and more and consume less because we as a country have got to export more and import less'. They tried that in Britain, but of course the same demand was made of the French workers, and the German workers and the American workers, and the workers of all the other Capitalist countries.

Now you don't have to be a profound economist to know that every country can't export more and import less. It all adds up to the classic conditions for recessions, for slump and crisis, and is the economics of the mad-house.

Socialism on the other hand is a system of society for the sole aim of production. It aims to create an abundance not for profit, but to satisfy human need. As production increases purchasing power, either directly through wages or indirectly through social wage, is expanded and we encourage every development available to known science and technology. So if some economist can double, or treble, or quadruple production per week, you will have a celebration, you will honour that economist or that team for their contribution towards humanity. Whereas it is arguable that in some Capitalist countries, and indeed in the Common Market, if somebody were to quadruple the production of eggs, you would say 'keep it quiet, destroy that secret, because you will wreak havoc with our Capitalist market'.

Socialist economies and socialist societies will plan in an expanding and developing way the utilisation of our wealth-producing resources. This does not apply only to the utilisation of technology: it also liberates the productive capacities and inventiveness of workers and of the labour force. Because workers in a Socialist society will have an invested interest in the expanding production and economy. In Capitalist society it is indeed possible to put forward new ideas on how to expand production – but one of the outcomes of your zeal will be to work yourself out of a job. That can't happen in a socialist society because as our capacity to produce expands, so our needs develop, and progress isn't expressed in a large pool of unemployed while the workers lucky enough to have a job are working forty hours. Instead we would merely be reducing the working week, the working day, increasing holidays and utilising everyone in the productive processes.

In addition, workers under Capitalism view labour through the eyes of people who are not their own masters. But in a Socialist Britain some worker who was outstanding in terms of production could be respected. In capitalist Britain, a man who goes pell-mell into the production of his machine and makes nonsense of the work rate of others, is quite frankly, not thought too highly of. The other workers look upon him as a bit of a horse. For example, in the yard where I worked we have a suggestions box on how to increase production. There was a man who had an idea for a change in the founding so that he could double his production. He put the proposal into the box and the management had a look at it. It was a simple proposal – sometimes the best ideas have a tremendous simplicity about them. When the experts came on the scene they said, 'yes, this is a winner'. So the man was praised to the heavens by his employer, as a good example of how people should be responding, and he got a cheque for £50. Then, some months after they introduced the idea, the management sent for us, and told us they wanted to declare redundancies in this sector of the machine shop. And that was the direct result of the application of this idea!

In a Socialist society there will be no such contradictions. Anyone and everyone who can suggest ways which ease the burden of labour but improve efficiency will be lauded, because the object of production will be to make life better, to satisfy all the material needs of the working people. And it is in this context that when you examine history, there can be no doubt – and this is what Communist philosophy teaches – that Socialism will triumph. It is an historical inevitability, not a mechanical inevitability. We can't all sit back and say Socialism will prevail, brought about by the operation of certain mechanical processes of history. History works through man. It's man in mankind, and people who determine history. So it's not only mechanical inevitability that the workers will fight for Socialism. I would say that it is also a political and psychological inevitability. As Capitalism becomes increasingly bankrupt, it will become more and more obvious that it can't unleash and utilise the wonders and scientific achievements of man in a creative and productive sense, but will ecologically destroy man's environment. Indeed it is the creed of Capitalism in many instances which has brought about all the problems that so concern the ecologists, and should concern the great mass of mankind. And it is in this context, this understanding of history, that we see the inevitable bankruptcy of Capitalism, and the consequential dynamism of Socialism as a system that will end the contradictions of Capitalism and open the door so that mankind may progress towards a new higher and better system of society.

This awareness gives every Socialist and every class-conscious worker the confidence, the knowledge that – whatever the ups-and-downs of the movement – there is no need to despair. Socialism will experience setbacks, but these setbacks are temporary. In the last analysis the future belongs to us – to all those who are fighting for a new society, for a better society, a Socialist society. That's why there is no despair among us, in spite of setbacks in different parts of the globe. During the Vietnam war, Socialists could predict only one outcome despite the technological superiority of the capitalist United States' forces. The heroic people of south-east Asia would defeat their enemy and win, because that's the process of contemporary history.

Now Communism is also a kind of society which doesn't exist anywhere in the world today. I hear people talking about Communist countries – Communists would never acknowledge that there exists a Communist state anywhere in the world today.

Socialism is a system of society where we end the exploitation of man by man. And the Socialist transformation of society involves political, economical and cultural changes which are the very essence of a Socialist revolution. Incidentally when we talk about a Socialist revolution, we are talking about fundamental change. That fundamental change can be effected in certain conditions through the ballot boxes, and without recourse to civil war. But in other countries where people are denied such basic rights then it may take another form. The maxim of a Socialist society is 'from each according to his ability, to each according to work done'. The reason this is that within a Socialist society the productive resources and capacities are not yet at a stage to create an abundance for *all* human needs. And secondly the people will still have many of the attitudes born of Capitalism, and will need material incentives to perform, to produce, to study for higher skills. The object will be to reward people for their greater contribution to society, or to the productive cycle, or for enhancing their skills in order that they may make a greater contribution.

Socialism then creates the conditions for a higher stage. And it is that higher stage which is meant by Communism, which will operate by the maxim 'from each according to his ability, to each according to their needs'. Now this can be realised first because economic developments will pave the way to a production of actual abundance. We don't want super-abundance because that would be destructive of resources and capacities and could be damaging in the future, but in a planned society we would produce enough for the satisfaction of all material human needs. That's the first point. Second, there will be a cultural change. You can change human nature. The most reactionary slogan of all is 'you can't change human nature'. A man does something mean and despicable, and somebody says: 'there you are, you can't change human nature'. But if a man does something good, something for the benefit of his fellow human beings, some act which could be self-sacrificial for the benefit of humanity, you don't find somebody saying, 'you can't change human nature'. The idea that human nature, people's attitude to life, is a static thing, is so much nonsense. I'm a father with three children, and I'm certain all parents have this experience. They go to the hospital to look at the new child. Now if someone started to say, 'Now look here, that is going to be a very mean and grasping human being. And that other one is going to be a bigot. And that one there is going to have an attitude that is either good or bad,' then you would call him a fool. Because you are not born with an attitude to life. We get our attitude to life, to money, all our values, from society, from our experiences in society. To a large extent therefore, our attitudes towards our fellow human beings are shaped by society.

In a capitalist society you get this insidious propaganda, 'I'm all right Jack'.

We have heard novelist Mickey Spillane: 'Yes, my hero is a moronic sexual pervert. The Private Eye who gets the solution to his problem, not on the basis of erudition or reasoning, but bludgeoning everyone into submission.'

It seems that the more expert you are in exploiting your fellow human beings in a capitalist society, the more honoured and respected you become. 'Look up to this man. He is a great man because he's made millions at the expense of the labour and often the misery of his fellow human beings.'

But Socialism will establish real values. Respect for your fellow human beings. Respect, above all, for your fellow human beings who serve the community and not themselves. For people who try to fill the treasure house of human needs, both cultural and material, in every respect and not to fill their own pockets. Let me illustrate my idea of the morality of Socialism. Take a young school teacher living in a capitalist society, and deep freeze her into a state of suspended animation for a hundred years. Then unfreeze her and say: 'Now here's a class, give them some test of their arithmetical skill.' So she goes in and says: 'A man buys a hundred oranges at 2p each and sells them at 10p each and what would he get?' And the class will reply, 'Six months in prison.' Because those children will have been taught that it is not a nice slick thing to profiteer at the expense of your fellow human beings. Exploitation of your fellows is not commendable. It is almost animal-like and man will develop beyond that level in the context of a socialist society and a socialist morality.

Therefore Socialism leads to vast economic developments, and to cultural, and what one could call spiritual changes in the attitudes of man. And new attitudes can prevail. For example, if man has an abundance of bread in his higher stage of Socialism called Communism, he won't require money to procure bread. He will say: 'I want a loaf of bread,' and that's it. People react to this kind of prophecy by saying, 'But if we didn't have to pay for bread, we would rush to the stores taking 20 loaves and run home to hide them. There would soon be scarcity and shortage.' That's viewing circumstance from the standpoint of a person born and bred in a capitalist society. But even within Capitalism, we have some examples of how the principle would operate. We don't pay for water when we go for a glass at the tap. We pay indirectly through rates. But then you always make that contribution, you always pay, even in a highly developed socialist or communist society. Nobody runs to the taps and fills up buckets of water and says, 'We're getting it for nothing,' and hoards it. Because, generally speaking, there is an abundance of water in this country. And so you go and take a glass of water when you want and turn off the tap. It is not abused. It's a recognition of the reality that it is there as and when required.

So in a highly developed socialist society we will develop into a newer stage with this new maxim, 'from each according to his ability, to each according to his need'. And all these factors will operate productive forces creating sufficiency for human needs, and the cultural changes, the changes in the attitudes of man. Changing anachronisms in human nature I don't really think *is* a fundamental change, I think it is the full flowering of the human personality, emerging from the darkness of class-ridden society into the light of the dawn of the new society of Socialism. It opens up the perspective towards this beautiful system of human personal relations that values each individual, but also values his or her service to fellow human beings.

And this basically is the socialist philosophy which is the product of our working-class movement. And it is an adventurous philosophy. Scientists in the physical sense can change the world, but we've got to make sure that science is used to change the world for the better. Not to break the laws of nature: not to endanger future generations. A sense of responsibility to man, to our fellow human beings, to our species and our physical world – scientists must have this. While in the political, economic and sociological organisation of man we can do as well. The two must go together. I happen to think it is the greatest cause in the world, a cause to which it is well worth dedicating whatever abilities and energies we possess.

THE BRITISH ROAD TO SOCIALISM

*Speech delivered to the Communist Party of Great Britain's
30th Congress, November 1967*

> You who will emerge from the flood in which we
> drowned, remember when you speak of our weak-
> nesses, the dark times that you escaped.
> For we went changing countries more often than
> shoes. Through the wars of the classes, despairing to
> see injustice only and no indignation.
> And yet we know hatred against baseness also
> distorts the features; rage against injustice also makes
> hoarse the voice. Alas, we who wished to prepare the
> world for friendliness could not ourselves be friendly.
> But you, when the time has come that man can be
> helper to man, remember us with indulgence.
>
> Bertolt Brecht

In 1950 Harry Pollitt introduced the first draft of the Communist Party's, *The British Road to Socialism*, with these
words:

> Such a programme would end our present living from
> hand to mouth stage, and correctly link up our fight for
> immediate demands with a clear perspective for the future.
> Immediate issues and generalisations about Socialism are not
> enough. Thinking people want a perspective. They want to
> see the line of march and the path ahead. We have to outline
> a programme for such.

Today this remains sound advice.

The initial decision to produce such a programme was of great significance.

It enabled the Communist Party, based as it is on a scientific socialist outlook, to help chart the course by which our Labour movement can achieve our common socialist objective. *The British Road to Socialism* is an indispensable contribution to this end.

More valid than ever perhaps in the light of events in the intervening years.

I should like to emphasise several major points.

The ever-deepening crisis of the British capitalist economy.

This crisis has not emerged in the last ten years; its roots go back for decades. Yet in the last few years it has reached such dimensions as to be the necessary starting point for any serious consideration of a new road for Britain. Mr Callaghan, like the Tories before him, will exhaust all expedients, and the crisis, like John Brown's soul, will go marching on.

Our imperialist past and the present imperialist base to our economy is the root cause of the crisis. I would advise Harold Wilson, who has boasted that he couldn't get beyond the first two pages of Marx's *Capital*, to have a go at R. Palme Dutt's *Crisis of Britain and the British Empire*. There he will find an analysis of the problem and the socialist solution that all his economic advisers and trained experts are incapable of providing.

Britain's was the imperialist parasitic economy par excellence. It depended for solvency on the tribute pouring into its coffers from the four corners of the earth.

Social Democracy collaborated with imperialism and sought to convince the British workers that they would benefit from this imperialist plunder.

Whatever crumbs fell to the workers were of little consequence when compared to the price that had to be paid, not only in wars and the cost of armaments, but in the retarded economic and social development of Britain. The capitalist class, solely concerned about their enrichment, acted on the basis: Why spend money to re-equip or modernise British industry when investments abroad could secure safer profits from the exploitation of cheap colonial labour?

The process of decline of Britain's basic industries like coal, ship-building, textiles and agriculture, had started.

All of this would be of academic interest if it were simply a matter of past history. It is not. It is present-day reality.

First, successive post-war Tory and Labour Governments have tried, and are trying, to continue as before in a world where socialism is becoming the decisive force, and where the national liberation movements of the peoples of Africa, Asia and Latin America surge forward.

The refusal to abandon the imperialist basis of the economy is expressed in – retaining the City of London as an international banking and financial centre; maintaining the pound sterling as an international reserve currency; permitting the continued outflow of capital investment and preserving a military presence abroad to protect investments. Once again, devaluation has resulted.

As a consequence, Britain is declining as a force in the capitalist world before the stronger United States and other capitalist economies.

So delicate and dependent is the British capitalist economy, that if at any time in the months ahead the dollar coughs, the pound will be stricken with bronchial convulsions. If a gnome falls out of his bed in Zurich, the reverberations shake the Treasury.

What solution is offered? The same medicine that has not only singularly failed in the past, but has also worsened the condition of the ailing economy. The prescription is as follows: take it out on the British working class, and try to increase the tribute from abroad through intensified neo-colonialist exploitation – thus leading of course to incessant conflict both here and abroad; everything to be sacrificed for the big monopolies; the economy to be further distorted – and so the piling up of problems.

Second, we must take into account the experiences of the latest right-wing Labour Government.

Right-wing Social Democracy has traditionally played the role of attempting to secure the position of capitalism, and administering it when the people have rejected the Tories. This was the role of the Labour Governments of 1929–31 and 1945–51. This, in essence, is the role of the present Labour Government.

In the deepening crisis of British imperialism the Wilson Government has not only to administer capitalism but to manoeuvre ever more desperately to try and save capitalism in its stage of chronic decline.

Harold Wilson has been acting in the interests of the City, the financial trusts and the big monopolies. This is strengthening the political grip of big business at a time when the people's interests require the weakening and indeed the breaking of this grip, and when circumstances are ripe for bringing this about.

When the electorate voted the Tories out after thirteen years of Conservative rule, they wanted a real change of policy. But the policies of the Wilson Government are playing into the hands of the Tory Party so that the Tories can now talk again of staging a political come-back.

In the draft of our programme we try to show that all this has led to a crisis of policy in our Labour movement. The solution of this crisis involves winning changes in policy. It also means breaking the power and control of the right wing.

Third, we have to take into account in the development of our programme, the impact of technological changes and their relevance to the case for Socialism.

John Gollan, in his splendid book *Socialism in the Sixties* has argued our case, the essence of which is summed up when he writes

... if the new scientific revolution is not to break down in disorder, a social revolution is needed. We require a social system to match the new scientific age. That social system we will show can only be Socialism.

The battle for left progressive policies is taking place against the background of large-scale technological changes in our industries. Technology, automation, cybernetics and their application represent a revolutionary change in industrial production.

The first industrial revolution was ruthlessly carried through in Britain in the interests of the rising capitalist class.

Many vast family fortunes were founded in this period. It also meant widespread deprivation and poverty for the great mass of the people.

Harold Wilson's electoral theme was that a Labour Government would more effectively carry through the technological revolution than the Tories.

'Modernise Britain' was the slogan. This objective is not in dispute. The issue is – in whose interests? Is the second industrial revolution to be ruthlessly carried through in the interests of the monopoly capitalist class, or in the interests of the people? Wilson has clearly opted for modernising Britain for the monopolies.

This means weakening the trade unions, strengthening the employers, encouraging still further growth of monopoly, pumping in public money where necessary for capital re-equipment, accompanied by the 'shake out', a euphemism for sacking workers, and holding down the wages of those remaining.

The British capitalist economy which, when faced with even a minute economic growth 'overheats', cannot accommodate the vast productive potential inherent in present-day technology and science. Only Socialism, which has the aim of producing an abundance, can utilise and harness its scientific revolution to the needs of the people.

Fourth, we have to re-examine and if possible develop the way forward to Socialism.

How do we get from here to there? In other words, start

now from the problems and issues of life itself to develop the new political alignments that will make possible our strategy for the advance to Socialism?

The essence of the real political struggle in Britain today, as distinct from the inconsequential verbal fisticuffs between the Government and the Tory Front Bench, is the people versus the monopolies. The conflict of interests between the giant big business and financial institutions and the great mass of the people is widely felt, if not always understood. It is moving thousands of people into action – industrial and professional workers and others. It is a class struggle. It involves not only economic and social issues, but our democratic rights.

Alongside the growing centralised economic power of the monopolies has gone the centralised political power of White-hall. The Cabinet has usurped powers that previously resided in the House of Commons. Almost every authority in the British Constitution has commented on this process, which it is interesting to note dates from the rise of imperialism in the last thirty years of the nineteenth century. As Bernard Crick in his book *Reform of Parliament* puts it ... 'The dominance of the House by the Executive is ... a produce of habits born in the Parnellite struggle'. Which serves to underline the truth of the Marxist principle that a nation that suppresses another, cannot itself be free.

Monopoly power is a menace to democracy. Lenin put it as follows:

> The political superstructure of the new economy, of monopoly capitalism (imperialism is monopoly capitalism), is the turn from democracy to political reaction. Democracy corresponds to free competition. Political reaction corresponds to monopoly.

So with the growth of imperialism and monopoly, the ruling class, maintaining the friction of Parliamentary control, steadily erodes the real powers of Parliament, while trans-ferring these to the Cabinet and to the higher echelons of the Civil Service.

This process has accelerated in the last decade. Today in Britain behind the façade and trappings of parliamentary debate, we have a monopoly capitalist state where the apparatus of national government is interwoven with the great monopolies and banks. It is an apparatus staffed at controlling points by people who, by birth and education, through training and career prospects, have loyalists to Capitalism; who have been conditioned to see their job as making Capitalism work, to regard Socialism as subversive.

The authority and responsibilities of local government have been whittled down by national government legislation. Now we can see the more open attack on the rights of the people: the anti-trade union clauses of the Prices and Incomes Act, the Cameron Report and the open invitation to employers to smash workshop organisation; the contrived, concerted clamour from Gunter, Wilson, Heath, Maudling, the press lords and TV tycoons, to create the atmosphere for introducing punitive laws against the trade unions and all workers engaged against the employers.

This conspiracy is carried into the Labour movement itself, where right-wing trade union leaders are attacking the democracy of their membership and the rights of Congressess and Conferences to decide policy.

Any capitalist state represents the rule of a minority over the majority. A monopoly capitalist state represents the rule of a tiny handful over a greater majority.

To defend and extend our democratic rights is part of the class fight against the monopolies. It is becoming inseparably linked with the economic struggle. For example, the fight for higher wages or for collective bargaining is increasingly bringing workers into conflict with government policy and legislation.

That is why we state our proposals for more democratic controls, both economic and political, to curb further in the short term the menace of monopoly power as part of the process that will eventually end it.

In this context we suggest many democratic reforms dealing

with more popular control of the mass media and other institutions.

It is here that we reiterate our demand that the national
aspirations of the Scottish and Welsh people for self-government must be met. This is not a socialist, but a democratic
demand. Our Party in Britain has not done enough to popular-
ise and make known its position on the national question in
these isles. This must be rectified, and particularly we should
fight to win the Labour movement to take a correct stand on
this issue.

As to the socialist future and the relation between the
peoples of England, Scotland and Wales, these the peoples will
decide. This could be federation or some other form of
relationship.

At the same time we must make it clear that the working
peoples of England, Scotland and Wales have a common enemy
and a common class interest. The unity of the British working
class is a necessity for defeating British monopoly capitalism
and winning the socialist future.

All the problems confronting the people of Britain come
from a common source – the rule of monopoly.

The people suffer the effects of this role in their daily life.
They can feel and understand the effects, while not yet fully
comprehending the cause. They are prepared, given leadership,
to engage in activity and struggle on a whole host of issues:
the fight for full employment and against redundancy, for
higher wages and trade union rights, against constantly rising
prices, rents and rates, against the attacks on the social
services.

The central issue still remains the fight for peace. A third
world war would be a disaster for Britain and the world. The
people of this country know this. The danger of war stems
from the nature of monopoly capitalism and its desire to
control in one way or another the territories of other peoples.
The war danger remains as long as imperialism exists. Yet war
is not inevitable: imperialist aggression can and must be
ended. Our draft reiterates the great truth of our epoch – that

the combined forces of the Socialist countries, and the developing emergent nations, the national liberation movements and the Labour and Left movements in the capitalist countries are powerful enough if they act resolutely to impose peace on imperialism.

The fight for peaceful coexistence, like the fight for democracy, is part of the class struggle of the peoples against monopoly capitalism and imperialism.

The main aggressive force in the world is American imperialism. The main issue in the fight for peace today, is bound up with the efforts of humanity to stop America's dirty war against the heroic people of Vietnam. Congress has already recorded its position in the emergency resolution.

There is little doubt that everything points to a mounting and sharpening class struggle.

The vital requirement is leadership – Left leadership. The task of the Left is to rouse and lead the people into battle to defend and advance their class interests. The various demands of different sections can be merged into a coherent, Left alternative policy to that pursued by the government. This will not be an end in itself, but the start of a process which can lift the struggle from actions against the effects of monopoly Capitalism, on to political action to end it and replace it by Socialism.

A main aim of the left, socialist, forces is to end the domination of the right-wing and its ideology in our Labour movement. To unite and weld our great working class into the solid foundation for a wider popular alliance of the people dedicated to the socialist transformation of Britain.

Implicit in our whole approach is that we Communists seek to advance to Socialism in company with all Left, progressive, socialist forces.

We cannot go alone – that we understand. We also understand that the logic of history, both here and abroad, tells anyone with ears to listen that neither is it possible to go it without the Communists.

Finally we feel it is necessary to develop the possibility in

Britain of the transition to socialism without recourse to civil war, through the mass movement and the use of Parliament.

The key question in the transition is how to wrest political power from the representatives of the monopolies, secure it in the hands of the working class and its allies and on that basis proceed to build a Socialist Britain.

In other words, to carry through a social revolution. To some people revolution is synonymous with barricades and civil war. It is even implied that to envisage another course is to violate the Marxist concept of revolution.

This is nonsense. Any analysis of the Marxist classics reveals that whether the socialist transition proceeds by violent or non-violent means is not an issue of principle, but is dependent on, and determined by, actual historical and political possibilities and the relationship of class forces, both national and international.

What has happened in the last ten years strengthens this conviction. Despite some setbacks, the forces have grown which make possible the realisation of our strategy.

The corollary of winning a non-violent transition is that it must be a democratic transition. Victories in the fight for democracy against the big monopoly trusts will enable us to work more effectively for the democratic transition to Socialism.

One feature here is the rights of other political parties under a Socialist Government. I want to quote from the draft as to where we should stand:

Democratically organised political parties will have the right to maintain their organisation, publications and propaganda even if hostile to socialism. With proportional representation, the electors will operate their choice fully by contrast with the present unrepresentative, and in effect, two-party system.

Elections will give the people the opportunity to discuss and modify policy and decide what government they want. A Socialist Government which bases its policies on popular interests and aspirations, takes full consultation in forming them, and explains them fully at every stage, can be confident of retaining the popular support, first won, for its programme. It will see it as a necessity both to lead and to accept popular guidance.

To argue otherwise is to have little or no confidence in the people.

The other aspect that we have developed is our concept of advancing to Socialism along with all socialist forces in the Labour Party and wider Labour movement.

The unity we seek to establish is not confined to the immediate struggle, but is an alliance to go over into Socialism, and will be the basis for the broad alliance of the British people.

What are the factors that make such a transition possible?

Internationally, the balance of forces has tilted decisively in favour of the socialist and progressive forces in the world, creating far more favourable conditions for the transition to Socialism than hitherto.

Here in Britain we have a working class which constitutes the great majority of the people. It is also highly organised with a long tradition of militant struggle. United, it can and will win, and is winning to its banner other sections of the community whose basic interests coincide with the working class and conflict with the monopolists.

Potentially this represents a force that is overwhelming.

The aim should be to confront the class enemy with such overwhelming forces that he has no alternative but to yield to the democratic will of the people.

Of course this will not be easy. It requires raising mass struggle, breaking the hold of the right-wing on the Labour movement and isolating the monopolists and the Tories.

As the draft puts it:

This will not be simple; there will be advances and setbacks – but it cannot be bypassed. In the era of state monopoly capitalism, above all, the crucial battle must be the battle for state power; and in that battle, the winning of a majority in Parliament, the supreme organ of representative power, is an essential step.

The strength of the popular movement, therefore, will be felt inside Parliament, while the strength built up within Parliament has growing repercussions outside – the one supports the other.

Such a socialist majority and Cabinet would restore full authority and power to the House of Commons. The socialist revolution will thus carry forward and develop all that is best in the democratic traditions of the British parliamentary system.

Many things in the programme of a socialist government are subjects of debate, but it will not be a socialist government unless it takes decisive measures to reconstruct and reform all the organs of state power, and staff all leading positions with people whose loyalty is to the working class and socialism.

Such a revolution enacted through the democratic will of the people will establish majority rule in form and content.

Socialist nationalisation will break the economic power of the rich and will enable the people to play a full part in planning and running the economy. The democratic content of everyday life will be immeasurably enriched.

A Socialist Britain will be a force for peace in the world. Its foreign policy will be based on respect for the rights of all peoples to self-determination and full independence.

It will dismantle the structure of neo-colonialist exploitation and replace it with relations of friendship, aid and mutually beneficial trading agreements.

To the peoples of former British colonies we will extend the hand of friendship instead of the mailed fist of imperialist oppression.

THE ROLE AND AIM OF THE COMMUNIST PARTY

It is clear that Socialism can only be achieved through rousing the widest sections of the people to the need for basic social change in Britain, and by winning their active participation in the fight for policies which can be shown to be in their best interests. As the draft states:

> This can only be done if there is a clear strategy and discipline on organised lines.
>
> Socialism has never been won in any country but under the disciplined organised leadership of parties with that clear aim and a clear understanding of the means to attain it.

The Communist Party is such a party, firmly based on a Marxist, socialist ideology and outlook.

Our Party has a proud record of activity and struggle on behalf of the British people. We are organised, we have a press and publications – we combine the struggle on immediate issues with the fight for Socialism. The strengthening of our Party and its influence is vital to the development of the entire Left in Britain.

Our aim of Socialism is shared by many members of the Labour Party and working-class movement. With a common aim, we have a common interest in unity and the co-ordination of our efforts.

This must involve joint efforts to end the barriers and bans imposed by the right-wing against the Communists. Their removal will benefit not only Communists, but all who are for Socialism.

The question of our Party's affiliation to the Labour Party has been raised.

I would make the following observations on this point:

The original conception of the Labour Party was of a federal union that would bring together the trade unions, co-operatives and socialist societies. This party, from its inception, has largely been controlled and dominated by the right-wing social

democrats. Right-wing strategy down through the years in refusing the affiliation of our Party, in imposing bans and
proscriptions against the Left, in disciplining and expelling
lefts and militants, was to change the federal structure and
transform it along the lines of a rigid, social democratic party
on the pattern evident in other European countries.

In 1946 the constitution of the Labour Party was changed to
rule out the future affiliation of our Party. For this reason we
have not placed, and do not place the question of affiliation as
a campaigning issue, and to do so would, in our view, be unreal
and divert attention from the most fruitful ways of developing
the left movement at the present time.

As for the future, we hold that the leadership of the Labour
Party is not the permanent property of the right wing. The
mass base of the party is the trade unions, composed of
workers whose elementary class interests conflict with the
political aims of the right-wing leaders.

Our Party, as an integral part of the Labour movement, plays
a major role in the struggle for left policies in that movement.
It is able to contribute all the more effectively to the left
struggle because it is an independent party, based on Marxism,
not subjected to the edicts of the right-wing.

As for our future association with the Labour Party, this will
be determined in the course of the struggle. But we think it
would be wrong to tie us to the view that it must be in the
form of affiliation.

Rather we suggest that we should be prepared to look at new
forms, especially in view of the implications of our Party being
bound or limited by the constitution of another party.

Our programme puts it correctly in terms of the developing
left struggle breaking right-wing control, and thus securing for
the Labour Party a vital role in the building of Socialism. A
stronger Communist Party is necessary to facilitate this process.

Of course we also want to see the circumstances maturing
which would make possible in this country a single united
party of the working class based on Marxism.

Our programme must become our lodestar. We must fight against any tendency to treat it as an icon before which we genuflect every now and again. It is not simply a statement of principles: it is a guide to action.

Marx has told us that an idea becomes a force when it grips the minds of the masses. So, too, with *The British Road to Socialism*.

Our programme is the road to Socialism and the path to real greatness for Britain.

Right-wing Labour and the Tories cling to Britain's Imperial Grandeur like a pathetic matinee idol to his press notices of yester-year. The world is passing them by. It's time the British people consigned them to where they belong – the pages of a history book.

The greatness we offer is in the splendour and dignity of the achievements of a Socialist Britain. Living in harmony with ourselves and in peace and co-operation with the peoples of the world.

THE CASE AGAINST THE SCOTTISH NATIONALIST PARTY

First published in the Morning Star, *February 1968.*

Breathes there the man with soul so dead,
Who never to himself hath said,
This is my own, my native land!

Sir Walter Scott

By whatever definition one cares to use, Scotland is a nation. The Scottish people have an absolute right to demand and receive self-government and realise their national aspirations.

The issue to be considered is how best to realise these aims. The starting point should be the irrefutable fact that if a referendum were held to determinine the feelings of the adult population, a considerable majority of the Scottish people would opt for some form of self-government.

What is needed is a movement that can unite the great mass of the Scottish people around the demand for a Scottish Parliament Now.

To be successful this must be based on what is potentially the most powerful force in Scotish life, the Scottish Labour movement.

A nationalist movement, unlike a Nationalist Party, does not require a political programme. Like the peace or anti-apartheid movements, or campaigns against higher rents or for comprehensive education, it can seek to unite people of differing political or philosophical views on a single issue – in this case, 'Home rule for Scotland'.

The Scottish Nationalist Party is a political party. In a Party publication issued in 1966 you read that until a Scottish parliament is won:

> ... SNP MPs will take part in the UK Parliament, voting and working in the interests of the people of Scotland, in support of legislation which is in accord with SNP policy.

The impression is widespread that the SNP is solely interested in winning a Scottish parliament. That it will then retire from the scene and leave the people to elect a government of the left or right according to popular feeling. In fairness to the leadership of the Party they have made it clear that this is not their intention.

> After freedom has been achieved as a result of massive support for the Nationalist Party, it will continue to contest elections on the basis of its policies for the social and economic welfare of the people of Scotland.

This being so it is necessary to look at this party's programme in the same way as we examine others. Is its policy left or right? Is is based on what will benefit the people or what will benefit the rich? It cannot do both. At the same time this party faces a dilemma based on a contradiction. It wants the benefits of being a movement that can win the support of both left and right, but as a political party it must have a programme that is either left or right.

This contradiction is irreconcilable. The result is a policy statement such as a publication called *Clearway Ahead* which has, as one of its slogans, 'No Left Turn, No Right Turn.'

What does this mean? That you go straight on? Current policies are taking us in a rightward direction. To go straight on would mean going further to the right. Consider Dr R. D. McIntyre, president of the Party, writing in an official Party publication:

> We deny the false doctrines of the Class War and of

Hereditary Ruling Castes, and we reject the false division of society which spring from both.

This has a familiar ring about it. Every right-wing theoretician who has tried to degut the Labour movement of its socialist class outlook, has expressed nearly similar sentiments.

Is it seriously suggested that there are no conflicting classes in Scotland? No exploiters and no exploited, only Scots?

The landed nobility is no figment of the imgination. It exists, and on the basis of false title deeds owns millions of acres of Scottish land. Feudal in outlook, it stands in the way of social progress, particularly in the Highlands.

The problem of the Clyde's shipbuilding industry in the thirties and in the sixties is not simply London rule, but Lithgow rule.

'Scotland First', is a neat slogan, but it begs the question, Which Scotland? As a product of the Scottish working class, I am more kith and kin with a London docker or a black African miner than with the Countess of Sutherland or Sir Alec Douglas Home.

In all the policy statements of the SNP there is no mention of Socialism. That might be considered an unfair criticism. However, I believe it is permissible because implicit in the policy statement is the concept of the continuance of Capitalism.

An SNP booklet entitled *The SNP and You* states:

Existing factories under English and other non-Scottish control, will not be subject to new restrictions. Owners will be free to make further investment and to draw interest and profit subject only to the payment of Scottish rates and taxes and to complying with the law regarding conditions of employment.

In the field of foreign affairs, the same underlying concept emerges.

The power and influence of the Western bloc of nations

would be strengthened, not weakened, if Scotland was independent.

And from Party chairman Arthur Donaldson:

> So long as the world situation is as at present, participation in the NATO defence system may remain necessary. As things are, Scotland is more complete serf or satellite of England, than Poland, Hungary and Bulgaria are of the USSR.

This concept of the socialist states of Eastern Europe as vassals of the Soviet Union is revealing. It is a concept which has long since been abandoned by the professional anti-communist hacks.

What conclusions do we draw from all this? First, that many members of the SNP are far from sharing the views and the outlook that underlie their policy statements.

Second that these members, socialist and progressive in outlook, must either fight to change these policies, or join a Party that stands for both Scottish self-government and Socialism . . . the Communist Party.

Third, that despite other differences, if the SNP, the Liberals, the Communist Party, the Scottish Labour Movement and all who believe in a Scottish parliament were to find common ground in pressing both inside and outside of Parliament, this would bring us nearer to victory than at any time in the last 250 years.

AN INTRODUCTION TO THE UCS CRISIS
1971–72

by Ruth Wishart

In 1971 there were only five shipyards left on the Upper Clyde, four in Glasgow itself and one in Clydebank. Fairfields and Stephens on the south bank, Connels and Yarrows on the north bank and Clydebank's John Browns made up the consortium known as Upper Clyde Shipbuilders, though Yarrows had already begun moves to go independent.

The yards had already seen massive redundancies, yet at the beginning of that year prospects had rarely seemed brighter. A lengthy list of unprofitable contracts had been finished, and a new order book full of sounder contracts had taken its place. Labour relations had improved out of all recognition from the days when demarcation was the name of the shipbuilding game.

The first clouds on an otherwise optimistic horizon appeared when the Tory government stopped its normal practice of guaranteeing owners against possible losses on UCS orders. And, of course, it had by then become acknowledged government policy to allow the liquidation of uncompetitive firms . . . a policy from which not even Rolls-Royce had been exempt. The government spokesman on such matters was John Davies, imported by Heath from industry, apparently to lend business expertise to Cabinet deliberations.

It was Davies' now infamous 'lame ducks' speech which spelt out the government's intention towards UCS. It would have been less of a shock to the men involved in UCS had they had earlier access to what became known as 'The Ridley

Memorandum'. This was a document penned by the then Opposition spokesman on technology, Nicholas Ridley, as far back as 1969. In it he recommended that UCS be carved up, by first hiving off Yarrows, and then selling what was left cheaply to private enterprise.

In February of 1971 the first steps were taken to bring this plan to fruition. Yarrows was extricated from the consortium, and given four and a half million pounds to re-launch it. Simultaneously Davies announced that no new public funds would be made available to UCS.

At that juncture nobody had asked for them.

But the effect of the statement was to create a four-deep queue of creditors at the door of UCS. The money quickly ran out and by June the management submitted a request for a further loan.

Davies turned them down flat.

Instead the government commissioned a report on the state of the company and appointed a committee which quickly became known as the 'Three Wise Men' ... later to be joined by a fourth. The names of the committee did not inspire a wave of confidence in the Clydeside workforce ... Alexander McDonald, chairman of Distillers; Sir Alexander Glen, shipping magnate; David MacDonald, director of merchant bankers Hill Samuel. And the fourth was Lord Robens!

These gentlemen recommended that the continuation of UCS would be wholly unjustified, and would cause serious and more widespread damage. They suggested a liquidation involving the loss of seven jobs in ten.

But by the time Davies announced their findings in the Commons on July 29th the workforce had made their own recommendations.

As soon as the management told them the position the leading shop stewards met in emergency session.

'We went through all the options and none of them fitted,' said Jimmy Reid. 'If we went on strike we would have to leave the yard and they would have closed it. It was as simple as that. If we had a sit-in strike it would appear negative. So gradually the concept of the work-in evolved, a concept where we could demonstrate we were really fighting for the right to work. And what better way to do that than by continuing to work?'

But first it was agreed to send a trainload of workers to London, and a deputation to see Heath. On the recommendation of the Provost of Clydebank, this was financed from the Common Good fund. Provost Robert Fleming made his position clear. He contended that Heath's government was attempting to do to Clydebank what the Nazis had failed to in the Second World War.

A delegation did meet Heath on June 15th, to be followed in quick succession by delegations from the STUC and the civic authorities. None met with any response.

'Our meeting lasted for an hour and a half,' Jimmy Reid remembers. 'We had gone into the yard and studied all the relevant documents and tried to become as knowledgeable as possible about our case. And when we started talking about Lloyds statistical reports and so forth we took him by surprise. There's no doubt that he hadn't been properly briefed.'

The stewards met other politicians involved. 'But I got the impression that we were talking to men who didn't care, who did not know what it means to stand in a dole queue, and worse, who didn't seem to care.'

But the West of Scotland public did care, as they illustrated at the first of two mass marches and demonstrations on June 24th. Over 100,000 stopped work for the day, and half that number marched to Glasgow Green.

Yet the Davies announcement the following month shocked both the workforce and the public at large. One paper described Clydebank on that day as 'a town in mourning'.

The following day the shop stewards took control of three yards. Weekly stewards' meetings were arranged during the work-in, but all major decisions were ratified at mass meetings. Just under 300 men were used as the basis for the work-in, and their weekly wages were meticulously made up just as if the management were still in control.

But while work progressed in the yards, a campaign to gain public support was mounted.

'We could not afford to become embattled within the yards, and we started a programme of meetings all over the country,' Jimmy Reid explains.

It was also decided to give the media complete access to every meeting.

The men who spoke at meetings may have used different words to state the men's case but they all emphasised the principal position: no redundancies and no closures.

'We could be flexible on anything else, on whatever solution might be suitable to the government, but that was not negotiable.

'If we weakened on that principle we were in trouble, and similarly if we appeared too doctrinaire as to the solution we were in trouble.'

Thus the work-in progressed, the leading stewards in constant negotiation with Sir John Eden and others, and the co-ordinating committee meeting daily to run the yards.

On August 18th a second march took place. It was a brilliantly hot day and one demonstrator said: 'No doubt whose side God's on.'

It is now estimated that a quarter of all Scottish workers downed tools in support on that day. 80,000 turned up in Glasgow's George Square, the starting point for the march. The slogans summed up the mood: 'Launch UCS – sink Heath.'

Marching along at the front were Vic Feather, Hugh Scanlon and Wedgwood Benn.

The loudest cheers came for Reid's declaration:

The workers of Britain are getting off their knees, getting on their feet and asserting their dignity. Asserting their abilities in a determined and disciplined way that they will have a say in the decision-making of this country. No one has the right to destroy the aspirations of young men or the security of old men. No one has the right to demand that people leave their countries if they want work.

We started off fighting for jobs, and in a matter of days we knew we were fighting for Scotland, and for the British working-class movement. The real power of this country has been forged today in Clydeside, and will be forged now in the pits, the factories, the yards and the offices. Once that force is given proper leadership – is disciplined and determined – there is no force in Britain, or indeed the world, that can stand against it.

As it continued, the work-in received mass support, not merely in financial terms, but from a complete cross-section of the Scottish community.

'Part of the reason was that before then nobody had known how to fight closures, and redundancy,' Reid says now. 'And it's not easy to fight them. What do you do? What can you do? Usually after the officials have left, all that's left for you is the question of who goes first. But here was a refusal to accept it, and a lot of workers started to stand a wee bit straighter thanks to UCS.'

As public meetings continued, and support mounted, Davies was sent back to Glasgow in an attempt to retrieve a public position for the government.

But it was an attempt that badly backfired, for by then even the businessmen in Scotland were outraged.

The TUC held its own enquiry into the UCS affair, and it was during this that Jimmy Reid was able to play the stewards' trump card . . . a copy of the Ridley document.

The terms of reference of the enquiry almost excluded it as evidence, but the stewards were able to distribute copies both to officials and to the Press.

It was a sensation. For it proved that credit had been withheld, and a liquidation forced, to conform to a plan drawn up even before the Tory government was returned to power. Copies were also given to every delegate at the TUC Congress a few weeks later. After that there was a continued momentum, and it was obvious the workforce had both the support and the money to carry the protest through.

By September, though, the government had come up with a new decision. They announced they would retain the Govan and Linthouse yards with a reduced workforce. Davies met the stewards in London and advised them to accept ... or they might find withdrawals of existing orders in the yard.

At a meeting on October 8th of all the work force, Jim Airlie, chairman of the Joint Shop Stewards Co-ordinating Committee, gave Davies his answer. In a fifteen-minute address, given without notes, he won a standing ovation.

> We will not bow before intimidation and blackmail. The Tories cannot allow ordinary people to express their hopes and aspirations. If UCS is defeated then men and women everywhere will be afraid to say 'we have rights'. But we will not fail the Labour movement. We will not fail the working class. Above all we will not fail ourselves. All four yards, the entire labour force, no redundancies.

By the end of 1971 two things were clear. The work-in would not crumble, and not just the workforce, but the public at large, were implacably opposed to the government's policies for Clydeside.

By the turn of the year no more was heard of seven-tenths redundancies, and no more was heard of the Four Wise Men. Instead another feasibility study was begun.

Lord Strathalmond made it clear that something like £20–30 million would be needed to get Govan Shipbuilders off the ground and the government did not demur.

Interest in Clydebank was now being shown from America, and the stewards and unions began talks, while the government did little more than spectate.

In the first weeks of January 1972, two union negotiators flew to Texas and asked that a representative of the Department of Trade and Industry should accompany them. They were turned down.

The union officials returned with a promise that the Americans would come over to inspect the Clydebank yard.

By February the outline of the final solution began to take shape . . . a reconstituted Govan Shipbuilders covering not two, but three yards, and an American buyer for the fourth at Clydebank.

And that was the essence of the Commons speech from a much subdued John Davies on February 28th.

He announced that the three yards coming under Govan Shipbuilders would be given £17 million to cover inherited losses, plus £18 million for capital development. At the same time he promised assistance to the buyer for Clydebank, Wayne Harbin of Marathon.

It was almost over. Not a drop of blood was spilled, not an arrest was made, no disturbances took place. The workers of Clydeside had fought for, and won, their right to work, in a bloodless industrial coup.

THE UCS CAMPAIGN

Three speeches

It has so happened in all ages of the world, that some have laboured, and others have without labour enjoyed a very large proportion of the fruit.
This is wrong and should not continue.

Abraham Lincoln

August 18th 1971. Eight weeks since the government decided the 'lame duck' of UCS would need drastic redundancies.

Eight weeks since the workers decide to begin their historic 'work-in'.

30,000 people join a march to Glasgow Green and hear Jimmy Reid give this pledge.

Today Scotland speaks. Not the Scotland of Edward Heath, Gordon Campbell, Sir Alec Douglas Home – of the Lairds and their lackeys.

They have never represented Scotland, the real Scotland, the Scotland of the working people.

No title, no rank, no establishment honour can compare with the privilege of belonging to the Scottish working class.

That is what I want to say on behalf of UCS workers to our brothers and sisters who have responded so magnificently to our call for help and solidarity.

Government action has projected us into the front rank of the battle against the policies of redundancies and closure.

THEY PICKED THE WRONG PEOPLE.

We stood firm and refused to retreat. We were prepared, of necessity, to stand on our own and fight alone.

But we were not alone.

Confident in our belief in our fellow workers, we told Heath and his government that this was the breaking point for the Scottish working classes .., indeed for the Scottish people.

There were those – and they were few – who counselled against a precipitate appeal to the workers. But the shop stewards believed that time was of the very essence. That for too long the fight against redundancies and closures had been confined to the morass of high-level negotiations. Meanwhile workers whose livelihoods were at stake stood waiting outside closed doors to be told at second hand whether they might work, or whether they would sign on at the Labour Exchange.

AND THE ANSWER, INVARIABLY, WAS THE DOLE QUEUE.

This time the workers and the shop stewards of UCS were determined this would not happen.

This time we took appropriate action and appealed over the heads of government and institutions.

We appealed to the highest authority in this land ... TO THE PEOPLE.

Already there was pent-up anger and frustration. Hopes had been dashed. There was despair at our apparent inability to influence and determine our own destiny. There were creeping redundancies.

It needed only a spark to ignite those feelings. To give them positive expression. We suggest that the workers of UCS have themselves provided that spark.

We are witnessing an eruption not of lava but of labour.

The labour of working men and women.

Let Mr Heath take note. Unless he and his colleagues are prepared to meet the urgent social needs of the people then this eruption will engulf both him and his government.

It is incredible, but the Downing Street mentality seems to

be: this government has lost confidence in the people – let's change the people.

Edward Heath, I tell you this. We are going to fight and we are not going to change. Either you will change, or we will change the government.

> *January 1972. A mass meeting is convened to re-affirm that no solution will be sought for UCS which does not involve the retention of all four yards in the UCS complex.*
>
> *Jimmy Reid puts the shop stewards' case.*

On behalf of the Co-ordinating Committee of the UCS Shop Stewards we wanted this opportunity of reporting to you on the stage reached in our fight. Because we believe that we are entering, indeed have entered, the most crucial part of this fight.

It's a situation where above all the unity of the work force must be maintained and the solidarity movement if anything has to be escalated. Because far too often in the working-class movement do we reach the crucial stage where victory is within our grasp, only, so to speak, to snatch defeat from the jaws of victory.

We say this because the situation is now a bit complicated, and more than complicated. Published reports of discussions and dialogues have created a totally false impression that the UCS crisis is nearing some kind of solution. But we say there will be no solution that is not consistent with the demands of the workers in the Scottish community and of the Confedera-tion of Shipbuilding and Engineering Unions. Demands for the four yards and for the total labour force within these yards.

If anybody thinks that we've involved ourselves in this historic fight – not only for shipbuilding but for Scotland – in order to sell the jobs of some of our fellow workers, in order to do some horse trading at the end of the day, then they have totally miscalculated the character and fighting capacity not only of the UCS shop stewards but of the workforce in the industry in the upper reaches of the Clyde.

Since our last meeting the movement has gathered new momentum. And both UCS and Plessey have become focal points in the struggle of the Scottish working class against policies that would render our communities economic and social deserts.

Since that meeting there has been tremendous development, leading to total unity among the workforce. Whatever our problems, whatever the conflicting reports, when the stewards have gone back to the workforce, the mandate has been repeated overwhelmingly. We have had votes like 8,000 to seven for the original demands of the movement. The workforce is absolutely united and we have been the recipients of the finest acts of solidarity from the Scottish working class, and indeed the British working class, that any group of workers have ever received.

Around the UCS there are wider implications in the fight against redundancies and closures. We saw the greatest public demonstrations of the working class this century in Scotland in that march to Glasgow Green, where it is estimated that 80,000 people participated and hundreds of thousands stopped work. That's what has been happening. And alongside that there was the dialogue in the first instance with the government. These were not negotiations. Because negotiations imply that redundancies and closures are negotiable on our part. They are not negotiable. Our stand has been that one of the great weaknesses in the trade union movement in recent years has been the preparedness to consider negotiations on redundancies.

With the demeaning spectacle that always accompanies that – discussions on who goes out the door first, who gets stabbed in the back, who gets sold out, what happens to the blood money of the workers whose jobs are lost. All the rest of the demeaning, undignified experiences we've seen far too much of, particularly in the West of Scotland in the last ten years.

So there were no negotiations with the government. There was a preparedness to talk, and we've indicated that we will talk to anybody, but no negotiations that carry implications of redundancies. We totally reject that. We reject the attitude and the mentality that lies behind it.

The government, in difficulties over implementing its White Paper proposals, which were for the butchery of the industry and a new company based in Govan and Linthouse. with a labour force of two and a half thousand, could find nobody willing to take up that proposal. Until two months ago when Mr Stenhouse emerged from the gloom and accepted that he should make a bid for the new company based on Govan Linthouse.

Now we made it clear then, and we will make it unequivically clear from this platform, that there will be no negotiations or meaningful discussions with Mr Stenhouse or anyone else in the absence of proposals which cover the four yards and the labour force in them.

Next we had the suggestion of a feasibility study for Scotstoun. Now Ken Douglas is the acting chairman of UCS, he was the vice-chairman. Douglas was the managing director of UCS. He knows in detail the position of the yards in this consortium and combine. And he does not require a feasibility study to show the potential of Scotstoun or anywhere else. If somebody wants to indulge in an exercise which could result in a face-saving position for the government, they can go ahead. But we are not hanging around and allowing this situation to become protracted, while the government hopes for a diminution in the support and solidarity of the UCS workers. That would put us in a weaker position than before.

We asked Mr Stenhouse if he would consider taking over the four yards. In an answer to the Press he said yes, given government aid and assistance. That was on the Thursday. On the Friday he saw John Davies and the idea was publicly repudiated by the Minister.

Part of the difficulty in our situation is that, quite frankly, a logical solution based on the four yards involves a loss of face on the part of the government, because of the public commitments made and decisions taken in June and July of last year. There is little doubt they never expected the reaction they got. And if we could turn the clock back six months for them, there is no doubt they would make any necessary money available in order to avoid the movement sparked off by UCS, which is now expanding into a fight for the right to work.

But they are committed to a public position. But we don't mind any face-saving as long as the yards and the jobs are maintained.

At the end of the day the considerations are loss of face for a government that was criminally wrong in the first instance, or jobs and families needlessly sacrificed. If these are the considerations then their face will have to be lost.

At the same time the government has quite clearly withheld the necessary guarantees for contracts that were secured by the old UCS and have tried to use this as a blackmailing gambit. A gambit to try and force us into recognition of, and negotiations with, Govan Shipbuilders in the absence of assurances about the four yards.

It must be stated here that in the discussions that took place at the Department of Trade and Industry with all the convenors present, the union position was made absolutely clear : full employment in all four yards of UCS.

Subsequently at York, with the Joint Shop Stewards of UCS all present, a decision was taken by the Confederation of Shipbuilding and Engineering Unions which has received insufficient public projection.

Yet that conference took an historic decision. A decision going beyond previous ones, which declared simply and sharply that the Confederation backed the shop stewards to the hilt – the four yards and every job.

So when we talk from this platform it's not just the shop stewards and the workers of UCS talking, but we are also talking with the fullest authority of the Confederation and for that matter the British Trade Union movement behind us.

We are reaching a crucial stage in this fight. This campaign can be successful but there is a need for optimism and confidence.

IT CAN BE WON.

But I tell you to win any fight you have to have the workers in the yard or the factory concerned resolved to fight to the end and win. In the absence of that you can get all the decisions you want but there can be no final victory.

We have this in abundance in UCS. No movement, no fractures, no cracks in the unity. Whatever is said and written in the future I've never seen a better bunch of fighters than the UCS workers have demonstrated themselves to be since the end of June of this year.

Victory is important not just for us. There is now a tremendous feeling of responsibility on our shoulders because we have become the symbol of the fight against policies of redundancies and closures.

Defeat, or a settlement tantamount to defeat, a compromise which means the selling out of jobs, will have a harmful effect on all these workers who have been inspired to fight redundancies and closures.

On the other hand, success in UCS will have a regenerating effect on the whole working-class movement. We have to say that, and we have to fight along these lines, because there is now little doubt that since the general election unemployment has been used as an instrument of government policy. They rejected an incomes policy, but the strategy obviously was to create such a pool of unemployment that would make an incomes policy unnecessary.

These people do not control this economy however. Having begun a process with the deliberate objective of creating mass unemployment, they are finding out that the creaky economy isn't like a car speeding downhill. You don't just slam on the brakes and it works.

For the brakes are not working. And they find they cannot stop and start this creaking economic vehicle at will for their own political ends.

So increasingly people have begun to understand the need for solidarity with the UCS workers and those in the forefront of this battle; the need to support them to a successful conclusion. In all the complexities, one thing has remained – and will remain – constant. A solution for the four yards and for the workforce. We have never been dogmatic about the form this solution should take.

As I said earlier if they want to devise a format that is a face-saving one then that is fair enough.

But we would argue that sensibly and economically the four yards should be maintained as an entity.

But if they offer to retain the yards in one company or two then we shall agree so long as our minimum requirements are met.

Don't forget the policy of the labour movement that when this government is defeated at the next general election – as it will be – one of the first proposals will be for the nationalisation of the shipbuilding industry. We want to ensure that there is still shipbuilding here on the Clyde to be brought into public ownership.

And let us hope that it is the kind of public ownership proposed in opposition by Tony Benn. A kind of nationalisation which will involve the workers in the running and control of their industry.

Just now we are in the midst of the woods. And there are wolves ready to pounce if we make a tactical error, if we turn our backs for a moment someone will jump on them.

It is a dangerous situation for us to be in. But it becomes less dangerous with the unity of the workforce, and the increased understanding of other sections of the working-class movement, particularly in Scotland. It is vital that this support is maintained and consolidated.

Let me say one final thing, brothers.

We have been in negotiations before with employers and with governments. And the strength of your position in negotiations is always the strength you have behind you. If you enter a decisive stage and that support begins to weaken, then your negotiating position is also weakened.

That is not our situation as of now . . . but we are not going to take any chances. Which is why we wanted the chance to convey to our fellow workers the need for an even greater increase in solidarity. Give us that and we are confident that we can sharpen this fight. That we can move from dialogue to establishing the conditions for negotiations.

Give us that, and we can start to lay the basis for an entirely new approach to economic policies hostile to us in this country today.

Give us that and I am confident that we will all benefit from the new avenues being explored by the trade union movement, to consider creatively raising to a new level the struggle of our movement for the new emergent demands. Among which, foremost, is the right to work.

September 21st 1972. The fourth and last yard has been saved by Marathon of America. But they insist on redundancies. For the first time the workers are seriously split. Some sections want to accept the Marathon terms.

A crisis meeting is convened to hear Jimmy Reid condemn any defections before victory is secure.

This is probably the most serious meeting that has taken place during the course of our magnificent campaign.

I just want to go briefly over what we have achieved in fourteen months by unity. In June of last year the shipbuilding industry in the Upper Clyde was to be butchered.

The outcome of the report from the Government's Four Wise Men was to be a shipbuilding complex on Govan. A complex with a maximum of two and a half thousand employed and with guidelines laid down which would have resulted in wages going down and conditions more akin to the nineteenth century for the workforce.

At that time we said that this government wasn't on, that no government will govern men, that we were going to demonstrate in our industry – because of what it meant, not only for ourselves but for our community – the right of the working people to work. We made it clear that on this occasion they were going to be faced with a fight, such as they had never seen before. Here on this river, yard after yard after yard has closed, and trade union officials have come in to try to negotiate. They always come back to us with the same advice, 'half a cake's better than none'. In the midst of this campaign right up till eight months ago, they were arguing precisely the same case when they wanted then to sell out Clydebank.

But the reality is, that when we have listened to these people over the years, it wasn't half a cake we were left with, it was crumbs!

And we were left scrabbling about for our share of the crumbs! We took a stand against it, and I want to say here and now that what we've achieved in the last fifteen months is written in a way which can never be erased. New, glorious pages in the working-class history of this country. Because we not only fought on the basis of unity within the yards, we fought articulately and intelligently in a public sense, and generated the greatest mass solidarity movement in the history of the working-class movement in this country.

In the course of this struggle virtually hundreds of thousands of pounds came into our funds to maintain the work-in. Money from groups of school children who held little sales at street corners, from old age pensioners, people in the arts, people in entertainment and above all from our fellow trade unionists throughout the country. Even trade unions in South Wales gave £1 per week for months, because they realised that the stand of UCS workers was so important. They knew if they won it, they would have recorded a unique and historic victory for the workers against redundancies and closures.

It is important to bear these things in mind when we are discussing the matters that are before this meeting, because I say that nobody inside or outside these yards has got any right to advocate or abandon their responsibilities, not only to their fellow workers in these yards but to the millions of men and women throughout Britain who stood a bit straighter as a result of our fight and who supported us all the way.

We owe it to them and to ourselves – and I'm saying it to those nearing the end of this campaign – that this campaign can and should only end, when every job is secured ... but every job.

We've won significant advances over this period, and we have reached this point. You've all heard the term, 'snatching victory from the jaws of defeat'. We must watch that we do not snatch defeat from the jaws of victory. At each stage we've stood together for fifteen months.

We've got a solution in Govan because it was based on the continuity of shipbuilding. And for the record, I want to say that whatever achievements have secured the jobs in Govan were not only the achievements of Govan workers but of all UCS workers and all the shop stewards.

I argue that I had as much to do with the fight for the securing of the yards in Govan, Linthouse and Scotstoun as any single shop steward in Govan.

But the new reality is that a week this Friday there can be anything from three to four hundred redundancies declared at Clydebank. But you knew from the start of this campaign we were not thinking or talking in terms of divisions, we were talking of all the workers in the four divisions of UCS without prejudice or without discrimination.

It is the opinion of the co-ordinating committee that only one attitude can be taken, and that is that there will be nobody going down the road next Friday. If it was good enough six months ago to say that they're not going down the road, that they are in the work-in – that commitment remains.

The promise to workers six or eight months ago in Govan, Linthouse and Scotstoun, is a privilege that must apply to these people in Clydebank next Friday night. Otherwise, it's a betrayal not only of our fellow workers but of the movement that sustained us over fifteen months. Now the situation has developed in recent weeks where sectional differences have emerged within the workforce of UCS, and it's no good anyone trying to sweep these under the carpet.

In my opinion, sectional differences within the working

class, no matter what they are based on, are always self-destruction for the working class. And that goes for colour, for creed, for religion or for class. As workers we've got to stand together and look upon each other as brothers. I only recognise one label and that is, fellow worker.

If we had done that consistently over fifty years, in my opinion, we would be living immeasurably better in Britain today. But differences have emerged and have to be recorded.

There was to be a mass meeting yesterday, a mass meeting with a quite clear decisive purpose of a total reaffirmation of the labour force in the four divisions. That we would stomach it together and fight for every job. That decision has never been rescinded over previous mass meetings, and we gave the promise that it never would be rescinded unless by the decision of a mass meeting of the workers of the four divisions.

But yesterday we were faced with the position where the boiler-makers in Govan had decided they were not attending the mass meeting. And (it has got to be understood) they were not attending the mass meeting because they wanted to opt out of the fight for the jobs. Because that mass meeting was not about filling up your pool for next Friday. It was simply to reaffirm the determined stand we were all in together. And therefore, having taken the decision not to attend a mass meeting, they were opting out of the fight. That was also the decision of the boiler-makers in Scotstoun. The co-ordinating committee met yesterday and took the decision that those sections who had opted out of the fight, had abandoned their fellow workers, were no longer members of the co-ordinating committee, and were no more involved in a work-in. And if they've got workers in the work-in, or members in the work-in, they can be responsible for their members.

Because the money that was given to us was given to men that were on public record as saying, 'Give us your support and we'll not let you down,' 'Give us your support and we'll fight as honourable, decent, principled men for all our fellow workers. Help record a victory and achievement, which would be doing a service to the whole working-class movement.'

So yesterday, the platers of Linthouse by a very narrow vote, decided that they wouldn't attend a mass meeting. All the boiler-makers at Scotstoun, all the boiler-makers at Govan and the crane-men at Govan, are all no longer involved in the co-ordinating committee. They abandoned the fight by their decision not to attend the mass meeting, and they were on their own. Because unity can be a spurious unity, unless it's based on principle. It's got to be based on an understanding that you're abiding by majority decisions. Anything less than that is kidology, and you don't get anywhere kidding yourselves on.

The decision of the co-ordinating committee yesterday was to convene a mass meeting today and to say, now, 'Those sections that want to stand up and be counted can do so here.' Coming here is a testimony of the fact that they are with us, that they're all in it together. And quite frankly when you're in a fight, the only people you want around you are people that are in it with you up to their neck and are going to stand by you.

Because if I am in a fight, I don't want somebody behind me, and at the crucial moment find a deadly stiletto is stuck in my back. You're better having such men in front of you, or away from you, because they're no damn good to you, when you're in a fight.

My understanding of attending this meeting today, is to stand by the decisions, taken consistently over the past fourteen to fifteen months. The welders from Linthouse are here. The engineers from Linthouse are here, and all the out-factories from Linthouse are here. All the out-factories from Scotstoun are here, and came to the meeting yesterday and told us that they had a mass meeting yesterday where they put it on record that they are supporting the fight. It happens to be a fight for the Clydebank workers, but they are fellow workers. Sections of the general workers from Linthouse are here and I welcome these brothers here today. Because we've got a fight on our hands. I want to make the point to them all that this mass meeting will reaffirm its determination to continue the work-in, whatever the difficulties and problems. For there are greater problems the other way. We will call upon the British trade union and Labour movement to tell them the fight is not over, and I'm convinced the money will come in. And do you know why? Because I was at the Brighton TUC and couldn't get moving for hundreds and hundreds of delegates wanting to come over and shake my hand. It wasn't my hand they were shaking, they wanted to shake the hands of the UCS workers, for they thought the fight was over. We told them it's not over. And they said they would do everything necessary to help us sustain our fight, to carry it to victory. So we've got to take a position to fight any shilly-shallying. We've got to re-introduce the levy, so that we're putting money into the kitty to sustain our workers over this period. And we're telling Marathon, and the government and the Confederation that we're men of our word. We will not budge from our original decision, which in all circumstances was an objective of necessity for the working people and the community in the West of Scotland. Let me make this last word of warning – unity is of the very essence so far as workers are concerned. Let me tell those workers who think they are fire-proof and are wanting to opt out, that the result of this meeting today cannot in any circumstances be a secret.

But let me say that most sections that are trying to get out of their fight now because they think they are secure, in my opinion are making a laughing stock of themselves and the British trade union movement.

Let them – as is certain – run into difficulties next year, and the year following, and let them go to the British working class and say, 'Give us your support and give us your solidarity,' and there will be laughter from Land's End to John o' Groats.

Because the finger will be pointed at them and they will be asked: 'What bloody right have you got to ask for support or solidarity, when at a crucial stage of the fight, you turned your backs on your fellow workers who stood shoulder to shoulder for fifteen months.'

That's the reality of the situation. Therefore what we want

from this meeting today, is for those of us that are here to reaffirm our position. We're re-introducing the 50p levy as from next week, we're telling Marathon that these bodies will be coming in this door and they had better maximise the jobs. We'll be on to the government, and we'll make a public appeal, not here in a begging sense, but an appeal in the sense that we have remained true throughout this fifteen months of struggle, that we want to win, and that we can win once again, given their support and their solidarity.

ALIENATION

Rectorial Address. Delivered by Jimmy Reid
at the University of Glasgow, April 1972,
at his installation as Rector.

> *A Rat Race Is For Rats. We are not rats. We are*
> *human beings.*
>
> Jimmy Reid, 1972

Alienation is the precise and correctly applied word for des-
cribing the major social problem in Britain today. People feel
alienated by society. In some intellectual circles it is treated
almost as a new phenomenon. It has, however, been with us
for years. What I believe to be true is that today it is more
widespread, more pervasive than ever before. Let me, right at
the outset, define what I mean by alienation. It is the cry of
men who feel themselves the victims of blind economic forces
beyond their control. It is the frustration of ordinary people
excluded from the processes of decision making. The feeling of
despair and hopelessness that pervades people who feel with
justification that they have no real say in shaping or deter-
mining their own destinies.

Many may not have rationalised it. May not even understand, may not be able to articulate it. But they feel it. It therefore conditions and colours their social attitudes. Alienation
expresses itself in different ways among different people. It is
to be found in what our courts often describe as 'the criminal
anti-social behaviour of a section of the community'. It is expressed by those young people who want to opt out of society,
by drop outs, the so-called maladjusted, those who seek to

escape permanently from the reality of society through intoxi-
cants and narcotics. Of course it would be wrong to say it was
the sole reason for these things. But it is a much greater factor
in all of them than is generally recognised.

Society and its prevailing sense of values leads to another
form of alienation. It alienates some from humanity. It parti-
ally de-humanises some people, makes them insensitive, ruth-
less in their handling of fellow human beings, self-centred and
grasping. The irony is, they are often considered normal and
well adjusted. It is my sincere contention that anyone who can
be totally adjusted to our society is in greater need of psy-
chiatric analysis and treatment than anyone else. They remind
one of the character in the novel, *Catch 22*, the father of Major
Major. He was a farmer in the American Mid-West. He hated
suggestions for things like Medi-care, social services, unemployment benefits or civil rights. He was, however, an enthusi-
ast for the agricultural policies that paid farmers for not bringing their fields under cultivation. From the money he got for
not growing alfalfa be bought more land in order not to grow
alfalfa. He became rich. Pilgrims came from all over the state
to sit at his feet and learn how to be a successful non-grower of
alfalfa. His philosophy was simple. The poor didn't work hard
enough and so they were poor. He believed that the good Lord
gave him two strong hands to grab as much as he could for
himself. He is a comic figure. But think – have you not met his
like here in Britain? Here in Scotland? I have.

It is easy and tempting to hate such people. However it is
wrong. They are as much products of society and a consequence of that society, human alienation, as the poor drop out.
They are losers. They have lost essential elements of our
common humanity. Man is a social being. Real fulfilment for
any person lies in service to his fellow men and women. The
big challenge to our civilisation is not Oz, a magazine I haven't
seen let alone read. Nor is it permissiveness, although I agree
our society is too permissive. Any society which, for example,
permits over one million people to be unemployed is far too
permissive for my liking. Nor is it moral laxity in the narrow

sense that this word is generally employed – although in a sense here we come nearer to the problem. It does involve morality, ethics and our concept of human values. The challenge we face is that of rooting out anything and everything that distorts and devalues human relations. Let me give two examples from contemporary experience to illustrate the point.

Recently on television I saw an advertisement. The scene is a banquet. A gentleman is on his feet proposing a toast. His speech is full of phrases like 'this full-bodied specimen'. Sitting beside him is a young, buxom woman. The image she projects is not pompous but foolish. She is visibly preening herself, believing that she is the object of this bloke's eulogy. Then he concludes – 'and now I give . . .' then a brand name of what used to be described as Empire sherry. The woman is shattered, hurt and embarrassed. Then the laughter. Derisive and cruel laughter. The real point, of course, is this: in this charade the viewers were obviously expected to identify not with the victim but with her tormentors.

The other illustration is the widespread, implicit acceptance of the concept and term, 'the rat race'. The picture it conjures up is one where we are scurrying around scrambling for position, trampling on others, back-stabbing, all in pursuit of personal success. Even genuinely intended friendly advice can sometimes take the form of someone saying to you, 'Listen, you look after number one.' Or as they say in London, 'Bang the bell, Jack, I'm on the bus.'

To the students I address this appeal. Reject these attitudes. Reject the values and false morality that underlie these attitudes. A rat race is for rats. We're not rats. We're human beings. Reject the insidious pressures in society that would blunt your critical faculties to all that is happening around you, that would caution silence in the face of injustice lest you jeopardise your chances of promotion and self-advancement. This is how it starts and, before you know where you are, you're a fully paid-up member of the rat-pack. The price is too high. It entails the loss of your dignity and human spirit. Or as

Christ puts it, 'What doth it profit a man if he gain the whole world and suffer the loss of his soul?'

Profit is the sole criterion used by the establishment to evaluate economic activity. From the rat race to lame ducks. The vocabulary in vogue is a give-away. It is more reminiscent of a human menagerie than human society. The power structures that have inevitably emerged from this approach threaten and undermine our hard-won democratic rights. The whole process is towards the centralisation and concentration of power in fewer and fewer hands. The facts are there for all who want to see. Giant monopoly companies and consortia dominate almost every branch of our economy. The men who wield effective control within these giants exercise a power over their fellow men which is frightening and is a negation of democracy.

Government by the people for the people becomes meaningless unless it includes major economic decision making by the people for the people. This is not simply an economic matter. In essence it is an ethical and moral question, for whoever takes the important economic decisions in society *ipso facto* determines the social priorities of that society.

From the Olympian heights of an executive suite, in an atmosphere where your success is judged by the extent to which you can maximise profits, the overwhelming tendency must be to see people as units for production, as indices in your accountants' books. To appreciate fully the inhumanity of this situation, you have to see the hurt and despair in the eyes of a man suddenly told he is redundant without provision made for suitable alternative employment – with the prospect in the West of Scotland, if he is in his late forties or fifties, of spending the rest of his life in the Labour Exchange. Someone, somewhere has decided he is unwanted, un-needed, and is to be thrown on the industrial scrap-heap. From the very depth of my being, I challenge the right of any man or any group of men, in business or in government, to tell a fellow human being that he or she is expendable.

The concentration of power in the economic field is matched

by the centralisation of decision making in the political institutions of society. The power of Parliament has undoubtedly been eroded over past decades with more and more authority being invested in the Executive. The power of local authorities has been and is being systematically undermined. The only justification I can see for local government is as a counter-balance to the centralised character of national government.

Local government is to be re-structured. What an opportunity, one would think, for de-centralising as much power as possible back to local communities. Instead the proposals are for centralising local government. It is once again a blue-print for bureaucracy, not democracy. If these proposals are implemented, in a few years when asked, 'Where do you come from?' I can reply: 'The Western Region.' It even sounds like a hospital board.

It stretches from Oban to Girvan and eastwards to include most of the Glasgow conurbation. As in other matters, I must ask the politicians who favour these proposals – where and how in your calculations did you quantify the value of a community? Of community life? Of a sense of belonging? Of the feeling of identification? These are rhetorical questions. I know the answers. Such human considerations do not feature in their thought processes.

Everything that is proposed from the establishment seems almost calculated to minimise the role of the people, to miniaturise man. I can understand how attractive this prospect must be to those at the top. Those of us who refuse to be pawns in their power game can be picked up by their bureaucratic tweezers and dropped in a filing cabinet under 'M' for malcontent or maladjusted. When you think of some of the high flats around us, it can hardly be an accident that they are as near as one could get to an architectural representation of a filing cabinet.

If modern technology requires greater and larger productive units, let us make our wealth-producing resources and potential subject to public control and to social accountability. Let us gear our society to social need, not personal greed. Given such creative re-orientation of society, there is no doubt in my mind that in a few years we could eradicate in our country the scourge of poverty, the underprivileged, slums and insecurity.

Even this is not enough. To measure social progress purely by material advance is not enough. Our aim must be the enrichment of the whole quality of life. It requires a social and cultural or, if you wish, a spiritual transformation of our country. A necessary part of this must be the restructuring of the institutions of government and, where necessary, the evolution of additional structures so as to involve the people in the decision making processes of our society. The so-called experts will tell you that this would be cumbersome or marginally inefficient. I am prepared to sacrifice a margin of efficiency for the value of the people's participation. Anyway, in the longer term, I reject this argument.

To unleash the latent potential of our people requires that we give them responsibility. The untapped resources of the North Sea are as nothing compared to the untapped resources of our people. I am convinced that the great mass of our people go through life without even a glimmer of what they could have contributed to their fellow human beings. This is a personal tragedy. It is a social crime. The flowering of each individual's personality and talents is the pre-condition for everyone's development.

In this context education has a vital role to play. If automation and technology is accompanied as it must be with full employment, then the leisure time available to man will be enormously increased. If that is so, then our whole concept of education must change. The whole object must be to equip and educate people for life, not solely for work or a profession. The creative use of leisure, in communion with and in service to our fellow human beings, can and must become an important element in self-fulfilment. Universities must be in the forefront of development, must meet social needs and not lag behind them. It is my earnest desire that this great University of Glasgow should be in the vanguard: initiating changes and setting the example for others to follow. Part of our educational process must be the involvement of all sections of the university on the governing bodies. The case for student representation is unanswerable. It is inevitable.

My conclusion is to re-affirm what I hope and certainly intend to be, the spirit permeating this address, which is an affirmation of faith in humanity. All that is good in man's heritage involves recognition of our common humanity, an unashamed acknowledgement that man is good by nature. Burns expressed it in a poem that technically was not his best, yet captured the spirit.

In 'Why should we idly waste our prime . . .'

The golden age, we'll then revive, each man will
*   be a brother,*
In harmony we all shall live and share the earth
*   together,*
In virtue trained, enlightened youth shall love
*   each fellow creature,*
And time shall surely prove the truth that man is
*   good by nature.*

It is my belief that all the factors to make a practical reality of such a world are maturing now. I would like to think that our generation took mankind some way along the road towards this goal. It's a goal worth fighting for.

ROBERT BURNS

The immortal memory
proposed by Jimmy Reid,
Radnor Park Bowling Club,
Clydebank, January 1974.

> *Man's inhumanity to man*
> *makes countless thousands mourn.*
>
> Robert Burns

Robert Burns was a great poet and songwriter. He was a good man, a man who – in the period and circumstances in which he lived – was on the side of social progress.

He was nothing more than that.

But then that it is a fitting epitaph for any man. I say this because the Burns Club Movement, and its product the Burns cult, has 'honoured' the name of Burns while trampling and besmirching his spirit.

They have perpetrated the myth of Robert Burns. They have concocted a picture of the poet's life which could easily have been scripted by the writers of those near-pornographic films on view in so many of our cinemas today.

As they see it his life was as follows:

Burns was an Ayrshire peasant and ploughman. Through divine intervention – though they are unclear as to why HE was selected by Divinity – he suddenly burst forth into song and penned the most beautiful poems known to man.

He was promiscuous and helped swell the population of Scotland by his illegitimate progeny. He fell in love with an angelic creature called Highland Mary, which relationship ended tragically and abortively. He was a drunkard, and cut short his life, and thus his career, through his addiction to 'John Barleycorn'.

Harold Robbins could easily have written the scenario. The only snag is – it's quite untrue!

But this picture of Burns pleases some people. The Philistines. It pleases the Philistine man whose thought processes rarely rise above his navel, and at stag nights one can envisage them quoting his bawdy Crochallan poems. All the while deriving a vicarious pleasure from what they imagine were Burns' crudities.

It pleases the Philistine woman, who no matter what she says, has a covert admiration for any man she considers a sexual athlete.

Burns has to be rescued from people like these. He deserves – he has earned – a better fate.

Was Burns merely an unlettered ploughman? It is true that in his times there was no systematic education for the children of the poor. But his father – not untypical of eighteenth-century Scots – had a tremendous respect for education. In this the Scots were probably in advance of any other nation in the world. Thus Robert Burns was sent to school for two years to young John Murdoch at Kirkoswald. He spent a further three weeks with Murdoch on French and one week on handwriting at Dalrymple.

This might well appear a drastically inadequate education. But think for a moment. The class was small, Murdoch was, by all accounts, a brilliant teacher. He introduced Burns to Milton, Gray, Shakespeare and others and commented that Burns soon developed a remarkable fluency and correctness of expression.

Estimates vary, but it is generally accepted that by any standards he had a wide vocabulary. In other words he was a highly literate man, as any reading of his books and prose will demonstrate.

Was he a drunkard? There is absolutely no evidence to suggest that he died as a consequence of over-indulgence in alcohol. Hogg, the Ettrick poet, when asked if Burns was a drunkard, replied: 'Nonsense. Burns was no more a drunkard than I am, nay I would take a bet that on average I drank double of what he did, and yet I am acknowledged both in Scotland and in England as a most temperate and cautious man, and so I am.'

Instead the evidence shows that Burns could not drink excessively. He didn't have the stomach for frequent binges. He was, however, a gregarious man. He was a convivial drinker, and if that's a crime, there are millions of criminals, myself included.

In many of his poems he praises social drinking. In some – like 'The Jolly Beggars' – he describes drunken orgies. But read that poem . . . it's more observation than participation.

The cause of Burns' early death is almost certainly explained by the circumstances of his upbringing. He was born on January 25th 1759, in a biggin only recently built by his father. The walls were streaming and dank, the poet tells us. Ten days after his birth, a storm blew the roof off. From a very young age he was out on the fields. Making ends meet meant back-breaking work for the whole family of a tenant farmer. It takes no great imagination to understand that such a childhood could lead to constitutional weaknesses that would manifest themselves in manhood.

Was Burns utterly unprincipled with women? Some well-intentioned people react to this question by going to the other extreme. The truth I reckon is that you could count on one hand the number of serious affairs Burns had with women. Compared to some more recent members of the *literati*, this almost makes him celibate.

From my reading I estimate he had fifteen children which proves he hadn't just a fertile literary imagination! But there is no need to apologise for Burns' relationship to the lassies. Consider the man from all contemporary reports.

He had a brilliant intellect, a great personality and was an outstanding conversationalist. Well-built, he had an imposing appearance, a magnificent head with eyes which shone when he was engaged in interesting conversation. 'Often have I met with associates of the poet, who told me how – in his better moods – Burns made the listener laugh at one moment and weep the next.' He loved music and dancing, cherished good company and fellowship.

Burns was attracted to women. He liked women. So do most men.

More to the point, women liked Burns. It's easy for a man to be a pillar of sexual puritanism when he is not quoted with 'the lassies'. He makes a virtue out of necessity. But Burns, like Byron, was pursued by the lassies. He didn't run hard. Gilbert, his brother, said that Robert 'was constantly the victim of some fair enslaver'. Gilbert was somewhat straitlaced, but note the terms 'victim' and 'fair enslaver'.

His first poem was a love poem. Burns himself said: 'I never had the heart, thought or inclination of turning poet till I got once heartily in love, and then rhyme and song were, in a manner, the spontaneous language of my heart.'

The poem was to Nellie Kirkpatrick, the daughter of the local blacksmith. It isn't a great poem, but it was written by a fifteen-year-old, and it gives a portent of his basic genius. There is a passage in it:

An' then there's something in her gait,
Gars any dress look well.

Burns could take the language of ordinary people and express it poetically.

To Robert Burns, sex was not a shameful matter. He could write:

The deities that I adore
are social peace and plenty.
I'd rather be the cause of one
Than be the death of twenty.

That is a value judgement of an intrinsically moral man. For his times Burns was progressive in his attitudes to women. He looked upon women as the intellectual equals of men. Read his correspondence to Maria Riddell and others in which he discoursed about philosophy, religion and politics. We, male chauvinist pigs apart, accept this as normal today – but it was not so in the eighteenth century.

In the nineteenth century, Mary Wollstonecraft, whose daughter was to marry the poet Shelley, wrote a book on the rights of women. It is interesting to note that Burns, in the previous century, could write:

While Europe's eye is fixed on mighty things;
The fate of empires and the fall of kings;
While quacks of state must each produce his plan;
And even children lisp The Rights of Man;
Amid this mighty fuss just let me mention
The Rights of Woman merit some attention.

We can only understand Burns and his works against the background of the times in which he lived. Scottish feudalism was breaking down. But there were still virtually thousands of slaves in Scotland. The 'Liberation Act' was not passed until three years after Burns' death. The dominant section of the ruling classes was the landed gentry. The peasantry as a class was dying out and being replaced by the tenant farmer. They had to pay exorbitant rents. Burns himself paid £90 a year for Mossgiel. Ploughmen received £4·40 a year. Fewer than ten per cent had the vote. Only 205 people in the Burgh of Ayr had the vote out of a population of 65,000. It was a time of social, political and – in embryonic form – industrial upheaval.

It was a revolutionary period. Twenty-three years before, at Glasgow University, James Watt had invented the rotary engine which gave a new impetus to the industrial revolution.

And during Burns' lifetime two world-shattering political revolutions took place ... the American and French Revolutions. Burns was an enthusiastic supporter of both, as his poems and writings reveal.

Liberty, Equality, Fraternity were words that were firing the imaginations of masses of people in almost every land. In Scotland there was the Reform Movement. Again Burns was a fervent supporter.

He attended the Convention of the People's Society in Edinburgh in December of 1792.

His writings show his commitment:

His ode to Washington had the lines . . .

In danger's hours still flaming in the van
Ye know, and dare maintain, The Royalty of Man.

And his 'Tree of Liberty', dedicated to the French Revolution, expresses the theme to which he returns again and again . . .

Without this tree, alake! this life
Is but a vale o' woe, man;
A scene o' sorrow mixed with strife,
Nae real joys we know, man.
We labour soon, we labour late,
To feed the titled knave, man;
And a' the comfort we're to get
Is that ayont the grave, man.

Wi' plenty o' sic trees, I trow,
The warld would live in peace, man;
The sword would help to mak a plough,
The din o' war wad cease, man.
Like brethern in a common cause
We'd on each other smile, man;
And equal rights, and equal laws
Was gladden every isle, man.

Then 'A Man's A Man For A' That', with that glorious ending:

Then let us pray that come it may
As come it will for a' that —

That sense and worth, o'er a' the earth
Shall bear the gree and a' that.
For a' that and a' that,
It's comin' yet for a' that;
That man to man the world o'er
Shall brithers be for a' that.

In Scotland at that time the Scottish Church had unprecedented prestige. It was, in its own way, the only forum with a democratic content. But elements called the 'auld lichts' – the reactionaries within the church – had degenerated into an ecclesiastical tyranny ... a Calvinist Gestapo. They didn't worship Christ. They were devil-worshippers. Their sermons were exclusively concerned with the fear of hell. They knew nothing of heaven and had apparently been taken on an exclusive tour of hell by Auld Nick himself.

Burns took them on, and chased the devil from the Scottish highways with laughter. At that time Holy Fairs used to be organised with teams of Calvinist ministers vying with each other to frighten the people with the horrors which lay in store for them in hell.

Burns used this as the theme for his poem 'The Holy Fair'.

But now the Lord's ain trumpet touts,
Till a' the hills are rairin'
And echoes back-return the shouts;
Black Russell is na spairin;
His piercing words, like Highlan' swords,
Divide the joints an' marrow;
His talk o' hell, whare devils dwell,
Our vera 'sauls does harrow'
  Wi' fright that day.

A vast unbottomed boundless pit,
Fill'd four o' lowrin brunstane,
Whase ragin' flame, an' scorchin heat,
Wad melt the hardest whunstane!

The half-asleep start up wi' fear,
An' think they hear it roarin,
When presently it does appear,
'Twas but some neebor snorin
    Asleep that day.

But the 'auld lichts' and the 'unco guid' also had their snoopers, Peeping Toms who reported adultery by church members to the Kirk.

The offenders were then required to sit on the penitent's stool in front of the congregation to be publicly humiliated. The number one nark was Willie Fisher. 'Holy Willie's Prayer' is, I think, one of the best poetical satires ever written. Far too often we mistake caricature for satire. If satire means anything, it means to take the actual arguments – the language of those satirised – and then, with a subtle juxtaposition of words, let them condemn themselves out of their own mouths. And the opening of the 'prayer' is pure unadulterated Calvinist theology . . .

O Thou that in the Heavens does dwell,
Wha, as it pleases best thysel,
Sends ane to heaven and ten to Hell
    A' for thy glory
And no for onie guid or ill
    They've done before thee.

It goes on to devastate the hypocrisy of the 'unco guid'. In fact it could be argued that Burns did more than almost all the eminent theologians to purify the Christian Church in Scotland.

His Christianity was beautiful. Here he comments on a religious parade of thanksgiving for a military victory.

Ye hypocrites! are these your pranks?
To murder men and give God thanks?
Desist for shame! Proceed no further;
God won't accept your thanks for murder.

Then his address to the 'unco guid' in which his tender appeal
for tolerance and understanding is truly poignant:

Then gently scan your brother man,
Still gentler sister woman;
Though they may gang a keenin wrang,
To step aside is human:
One point must still be greatly dark,
The moving WHY they do it;
And just as lamely can ye mark,
How far, perhaps, they rue it.

Who made the heart, 'tis He alone
Decidedly can try us,
He knows each chord its various tone,
Each spring its various bias;
Then at the balance let's be mute,
We never can adjust it;
What's done we partly may compute,
But know not what's resisted.

Almost everything touched by Burns in his work is imbued
with a love of life, his fellow man and nature.

He took Scottish poetry and folk songs in particular and
raised them to a new height. Many Scottish songs would have
been lost in obscurity but for Burns. It was a labour of love to
him to take traditional Scottish songs and pen new lyrics. He
has left us a treasure house of songs as rich as any nation's in
the world ... 'My love is like a red, red rose', 'John Anderson
my Jo John', 'Ae Fond Kiss', 'Auld Lang Syne' are only a few.

Burns came from the Scottish people. And he expressed the
hopes, the aspirations, the dreams, the joys, the tragedies of his
own people in their own language. To the extent that he
succeeded in this he became a truly international poet. For the
great truth is that in being true to your own people you are
true to the people of all nations.

Burns came from a living school of Scottish poetry. He knew

this. His debt to Ferguson, he passionately acknowledged.

The cult of Burns almost killed the school of Scottish poetry. The Philistines have tried to deify a man who was not only conscious but proud of common humanity. That his name and works should have been used to discourage future generations was a crime that he would have found difficult to forgive. Only this century have we seen the significant emergence of a renaissance in our poetry with Hugh McDiarmid and others. Ironically I also believe that Burns made a contribution to the great English school of romantic poetry. Certainly Byron and Shelley were aware of his work.

His philosophy is best expressed in his own words:

Whatever mitigates the woes or increases the happiness of others, this is my criterion of goodness. And whatever injures society at large, or any individual in it, this is my measure of iniquity.

Such a man does not need mawkish sentimentality to perpetuate his memory.

THE CASE FOR NATIONALISM

Speech delivered during the October 1974 election.

Nationalism and internationalism are terms often used by people who haven't taken the trouble to find out what they mean. The resulting confusion is hardly surprising. In the trade union movement for instance there are people who state: 'I am an internationalist, not a nationalist.' This is understandable. The Labour movement, particularly the Left, has correctly enshrined the principle of internationalism. Nevertheless this statement is both wrong and quite illogical.

An international football match is a game played between teams from two nations. The prefix inter- means between, and nationalism is consciousness of the nation to which you belong. Thus if there were no such thing as a nationalist, there could not be an internationalist.

In working-class terms of course internationalism means the unity and solidarity of workers from different nations.

But nationalism is a term misunderstood and confused with jingoism, with master-race theories and everything else used by scoundrels down through the years to condition the minds of people against their brothers and sisters in other countries.

But this is chauvinism, a distortion of nationalism which is essentially racist. Whereas a healthy nationalism – a love of all that is good in the history and tradition of your own people – is the true basis of internationalism.

What then is nationalism? One thing is certain, it springs from a sense of national identity. It is a people identifying itself with a national entity, a nation. The more fundamental question is: what is a nation? Communists, socialists and the

Left as a whole, must attempt a definition. For the under-estimation of the national factor has caused considerable difficulty in the international working-class movement.

It is also important for the politics of the Labour movement in Britain itself. The argument of the right-wing that there is no nationalist problem in Britain is untenable. Continued neglect of this issue will be extremely damaging to the Labour movement.

An approach to the nationalist question requires a principled analysis. But unfortunately the Labour Party seems to view it tactically. Their response is dictated exclusively by electoral considerations. The SNP poll well in an election, and you can almost hear the thought process clicking ... how can we spike the nationalist guns the next time?

The real issue is not that, but how do we resolve the national problem? This involves ideological clarity. The precise defini-tion of a nation. It is a complex question, for nations are not static, they are not fixed points. At this moment in history there are nations being born, on the continent of Africa for instance. Like all other phenomena, a nation has a beginning, a life and development. It can also have an end.

So let us begin with what previous researchers have deemed the characteristics of a nation, and qualify them where neces-sary.

A nation is a specific community of people. It is not racial, for races can straddle nations. We can thank providence that there does not exist the 'racially pure' nation. Let us remember Defoe's poem, 'The True-Born English Gentleman.'

The customs, surnames, languages and manners,
Of all these nations are their own explainers,
Whose relics are so lasting and so strong
They ha' left a shibboleth upon our tongue
By which with easy search you may distinguish
Your Roman–Saxon–Danish–Norman–English

Neither is a nation tribal. The Scottish clans were not and

could not be nations. A nation is an historically evolved community of people. It is not a casual or loose conglomeration of people. I was re-reading the *History of the Italian Republics*. It is interesting that though they were not nations, they were important factors in the historic process towards the Italian nation. In a certain sense, a nation as we know it, is a modern historical phenomenon.

A nation is a stable community of people. This should not be confused with a stable population. There can be a population which in many ways is a stable community within a state encompassing many nations – for example the USSR. And, I would argue, Great Britain.

A common language is a feature of a nation. Not necessarily a language peculiar or exclusive to the people of that nation. Australia, Canada, New Zealand and the USA have a common language while retaining individual nationhood. So too with Brazil and Portugal.

A nation must be a territorial entity. The Scots may emigrate to Canada or Australia and the first generation of settlers may justifiably consider themselves a national minority. But with each succeeding generation comes the assimilation into the community of people historically evolving in the territory to which they have moved. They have become part of the historical process of nationhood.

Yet the mere fact of belonging to a territory does not make a community a nation. A nation requires an internal economic bond to bring together the various areas into a single entity.

A nation is therefore also an economic community. Nations as we know them today seem to be products of the industrial revolutions and of the economic and political developments unleashed by them. And although economics do not make a nation, without this economic bond there cannot be a nation.

Yet there is still something missing. A nation also has a spiritual complexion. The specific conditions of life, the specific historical experience, manifests itself in a distinctive national psychological make-up. A distinctive national culture resulting in a national character.

This is not to suggest that one national character is better than another. Simply that they differ. It is impossible for it to be otherwise. How could it be possible for the Chinese, the French, the Americans and the Zambians to share a national character? The infinite variety of national characters and cultures enriches all humanity. Long may it continue.

Collating these elements we can say that a nation is an historically constituted, stable community of people formed on the basis of common language, common territory, economic life and psychological make-up expressed in a common culture. It's some kind of definition. Probably incomplete and perhaps in need of modification in the light of further experience and further research.

How does this relate to nationhood in a Scottish context? Is Scotland a nation? Quite categorically it is.

From the sixth century there has always been a Scottish people. From the end of the tenth century, the territorial boundaries have been practically the same as they are today.

From the beginning of the eleventh century, we have seen the emergence of Scotland as an entity by the amalgamation of regions and principalities bound by, albeit primitive, economic ties.

Scotland was a completely independent nation. It developed its own constitutional form of parliament and this survives to the present. Scottish Law differs in certain aspects from that practised in other parts of the United Kingdom.

Scotland is a nation, and its history and traditions conform to any definition of nationhood that I've heard.

But every national question has got to be examined specifically. And two factors emerge from examining the national question in Scotland, and, for that matter, in Britain.

The first is recognition that Scotland IS a nation. And the second is that she is a nation which has been economically and politically integrated with other nations in these Isles for well over 250 years.

These are the two threads which must not be lost sight of in trying to resolve the existence of a national problem in Britain.

The facts are these. In 1707 there was a Treaty of Union. Legally at least it was a union, and not a takeover of Scotland by England. But over the two centuries it has happened – as it does with mergers – that the larger area has become the dominant partner. This is inevitable unless conscious steps are taken to safeguard the interests of the smaller section or nation.

It is also a matter of historial fact that this Treaty was opposed by a majority of the Scottish people. The Convention of Royal Burghs voted against it. There were popular demonstrations of opposition in all the principal towns and cities.

The Treaty was seen as an act of betrayal on the part of the Scottish aristocracy who had become very much absorbed and assimilated by their counterparts in England.

It is a fact that the Scottish court moved south! And it was a measure of snobbery for the Scottish ruling class to send their sons to English public schools. There they learned to speak like English gentlemen.

Even Burns, when he visited Edinburgh at the height of his career, was advised to stop writing poetry in his native lallans. Fortunately Burns refused to take this advice – or probably he couldn't write in anything other than his own language – and it is one of the great ironies that he went on to become one of the truly international poets.

The Treaty of Union set out that at all times there would be neither England nor Scotland but Great Britain: an interesting example of bureaucrats and so-called statesmen imagining that they can obliterate reality with a stroke of the pen.

For here we are in the 1970s and Scotland is still a nation. England is still a nation. And the reality from which we must start is that different nations do exist in Britain, albeit nations which have been politically and economically integrated.

The other factor of great relevance is that since the Treaty we have had the advent both of the industrial revolution and of capitalism.

It is the fashion to attribute all Scotland's ills to neglect from a London-based government, or a great conspiracy of the

English people as a whole to undermine Scotland's nationhood, Scotland's industry and Scotland's economy.

In truth the development of capitalism in Britain was preceded by what economists call the period of primitive accumulation of capital.

In Scotland the form this took became known as the Highland Clearances. But it was the Scottish landowners, the Scottish nobility, the Scottish aristocracy who realised the profitability of sheep with the emergence of a textile industry, and who carried through the rape of the Highlands. They cleared the Highlands of people, of clansmen and their families, and they plundered the land of the Scottish people.

A notable case was that of the Sutherlands. This family used soldiers and forged title deeds in order to steal the common land of the people. They annexed something of the order of 794,000 acres which had, from time immemorial, belonged to the clan, and to the people. And much of Scotland is still owned by people whose claims are not only spurious but illegal.

Second, industry in Scotland developed along the lines of heavy industry ... coal, steel, shipbuilding. This could be explained geographically. We had coal, we had rivers, and with coal, steel and rivers we had shipbuilding.

Now at an earlier stage of the development of capitalism this worked to the relative advantage of those areas where the economy was based on heavy industry.

But after the First World War, when Capitalism really developed, the crisis began which has reached chronic proportions today. And with the advent of the crisis, those areas based on heavy industry suffered, relatively speaking, worse than elsewhere. For when there was an upturn in the economy it benefited above all the light consumer-goods industries since they required less expensive injections of capital.

Thus, in those areas dependent on heavy industry, there was a continually high level of unemployment. It created considerable human and social problems in many parts of Scotland, and in parts of England.

So for thirty or forty years in Scotland we have had the situation where people have been driven to uproot themselves by economic circumstances from their communities, from their land and from their nation.

They have had to go to search for work elsewhere. The Highland Clearances were carried out in Scotland by the nobility ... openly, brazenly, ruthlessly.

But what capitalism has done this century has been virtually to occasion a Lowland Clearance. This time they didn't require legal battles. They didn't require troops to drive the people from Scotland ... instead they provided an economic whiplash.

Today this has been almost sanctified in a term called 'the mobility of labour'.

And so workers and their families have had to respond to the blind economic forces of capitalism.

This has been the pattern in Scotland for the last half century.

It is also true, of course, of some parts of England.

There is one difference – and this is not to minimise the social hardships and the price paid by working-class families in parts of England – but in Scotland there is an added dimension.

While you are exporting people – and it's almost by definition young people who are prepared to respond to the challenge of having no prospects among their own people – you start a process which, if it continues unchecked, is not merely harship but could become genocidal. It could lead to the destruction of the Scottish nation. Therefore, alongside the economic arguments for a reversal of this trend in Scotland goes the additional social and national argument.

We must have new policies in Scotland to reverse the trend and to preserve our culture and our nationhood.

It is against this background that one can argue very strongly for the recognition of Scotland as a nation. That there must be governmental changes in Britain which would allow for a Scottish parliament or a Scottish assembly. This is the legitimate and democratic right of the Scottish people.

Second, there must be a unity within the Scottish people – not only a unity of Scots, but a unity with the other working people within the British isles ... against the common enemy. No English worker can be the enemy of the Scottish worker. We have more in common with the London dockers, with the Lancastrian textile workers, with the Yorkshire miners than we have with the Duke of Sutherland, the Marquis of Bute and Sir Alec Douglas Home.

Our class identity is an important factor in the struggle for our democratic rights within society, and our national rights within society. We must have unity with the working classes of England, Ireland and Wales in our fight for a better life and for a better society which will correspond to our interests and our needs.

Above all the Scottish working class and the Labour movement has got to face up to the demands of the nationalist movement in a principled manner. The pioneers of the Labour movement were always in favour of a Scottish parliament. At the Labour Party conference in 1948 – when that party lurched disastrously to the right and created the climate for the return of the Tories in 1951 – Herbert Morrison argued for dropping the demand for a Scottish parliament.

This was carried.

The Labour movement has paid for that wrong decision. Just like the aristocrats who framed the Treaty of Union, Labour leaders cannot obliterate reality. All they did then was to create a vacuum in relation to the aspirations of the Scottish people for their national rights and their national identity.

A vacuum must be filled, and it *was* filled by nationalists in a Nationalist Party that does not in any conscious way relate to the most dynamic potent force for change in Scotland – the Scottish Labour movement. And a Nationalism which is abstracted from the Labour movement, from Socialism, must have within it the dangers of right-wing populism. This could be disastrous for the Scottish working class and the Scottish people as a whole.

What has not been helpful has been the opportunist manner

in which Labour leaders have responded to the electoral successes of the Nationalist Party. From a position of total opposition to any form of devolution we suddenly had instant converts. Clearly a reaction to election results and widely seen as a tactical electioneering response. The Labour movement should not be indulging in such acrobatics. It is not the way for the Labour Party to proceed on *any* issue.

The pioneers were right. They knew that an integral part of the Party's programme, both in Scotland and Britain, must be to realise the national aspirations of both the Scots and the Welsh; to make provision for Scottish and Welsh parliaments, while recognising the need for a strengthened unity between the nations of this island.

CHRISTIANITY AND COMMUNISM

An essay, 1975.

Merely to deny religion is futile. It is a dialectical result of man's essential nature being negated by material conditions of life.

Karl Marx

If a man claims to be a Christian, for Christ's sake let him be a good one.

Down through the ages, some men have paid homage to the name of Christ, while betraying his spirit and his teachings.

Christianity, or more precisely Churchianity, has almost become an empty husk.

Ritualised and formalised, without any meaningful content. A citadel of political and social conformity, respectable beyond belief.

Rationalists, freethinkers, atheists and others protest that the media, particularly television, give no time for them to advocate their opinions. They say it is full of Christian propaganda. They're either daft, or speaking with tongues planted firmly in their cheeks.

Television has plenty of insidious anti-Christian material. It has programmes like 'The Epilogue', 'Late Call' and 'Stars on Sunday'.

Poor Jesus. Not satisfied with crucifying him once, the Pharisees do so again and again. Spiritually and ideologically every night on the box and at least twice on Sundays.

It is difficult to combat the real anti-Christ in our midst, for it operates in the name of Christianity. And the Christ they project is effete. He goes through life preaching ethereal love and abstract goodness. A political conformist who accepts the class structures and privileges of his time. And all of this suffused in a spurious candy-floss piety.

This Christ seems to exist exclusively for the instruction of the poor. The rich and powerful 'Christians' – the aristocrats, landowners, bankers, financiers, industrialists, politicians and military commanders – have never been inhibited by a surfeit of such piety and meekness.

As history demonstrates, instead of turning the other cheek, they are more likely to instruct their paid henchmen to cleave off the offending hand. Or even head.

But where is the political conformity or class neutrality of a man who said, 'how hardly shall they who have riches enter the kingdom of God. For it is easier for a camel to go through a needle's eye, than for a rich man to enter into the kingdom of God.'

And where is the effete piety in the outraged Jesus who 'went into the temple of God, and cast out all them that sold and bought in the temple, and overthrew the tables of the moneychangers'.

Agnostics and others who think of Christianity solely in terms of the Inquisition, the torturers and the burning of heretics, the plundering crusaders and the bloody wars between Christian nations, are in grave error.

These phenomena were not the result of Christianity. They were the product of social and economic forces which used the banner of Christianity. It is true that the church did little to stop its name being besmirched, but that is another matter.

But this is only a part of the picture. Christianity and Christians have also played a liberating role in history. John Ball, one of the leaders of the peasants' revolt in England, was a priest. Christians played a part in the American and French Revolutions. Today, in almost every corner of the globe, Christians and clergymen of all denominations are fulfilling a significant role in the fight against oppression, privilege and the exploitation of man by man.

In Latin America and Spain, many of them lie in prisons beside Socialists and Communists because they are Christian socialists and communists.

Therefore, to think of Christianity as being homogeneously reactionary is dogmatist and a patent nonsense.

Dogmatists are the intellectual deadwood of humanity. A dogmatist's mind is closed. A closed mind cannot receive new information. A mind that cannot receive, and therefore perceive, cannot think. A dogmatist is useless.

No baby is a dogmatist. Dogmatism is inculcated by adults. Let me give you two examples from my experience as a father.

At one time my wife and I lived in London. My eldest daughter, then about four, attended an LCC nursery school.

Almost every day she would tell us how fond she was of a particular lady assistant there. On one occasion I took her to school and saw about five of these assistants, each wearing a different coloured apron presumably to indicate the groups for whom they were responsible.

I asked Eileen which was the lady she liked so much. She promptly said: 'the one in the yellow apron'.

It happened that the one in the yellow apron was a large black lady. But my child identified her by the colour of her apron rather than the shade of her pigmentation.

Conclusion: no person is born a racist.

Later we moved to Clydebank, where she was enrolled in the local state school. Being rather hard up at the time, we sent her off in the blazer she had worn to the London school. She came home crying from her first day. And she asked us in a bewildered fashion, 'What's a Catholic?' It emerged that the blue blazer she wore was the uniform of the local Catholic school. 'I didn't know there were Catholics and Protestants,' she complained. 'I thought there were only Christians.'

Conclusion as before: no child is born a bigot.

Since that day I have opposed religiously segregated schooling.

I am tired of Christian and even Communist dogmatists

quoting Marx as having written: 'religion is the opium of the people'.

He did write that. But as it stands it is torn out of context. For Marx had no simplistic anthropological critique of religion. He approached it as a part of his general critique of society.

Here is the full paragraph in question;

> Religious suffering is at the same time an expresion of real suffering, and a protest against real suffering. Religion is the sigh of the oppressed creature, the sentiment of a heartless world, and the soul of soul-less conditions. It is the opium of the people.

This is the formulation of a man who is not religious, but who views religion in a social context. It is not unsympathetic. I think that progressive Christian theologians can benefit from his contributions to the sociological development of Christianity.

To go further – the modern ecumenical movement would gain enormously from his analysis of the social and economic factors that played an important part in bringing about the divisions within Christianity.

Marx strove to provide man with tools and instruments with which he could both understand the world and make it better. These instruments are not perfect. They have been, and will be, modified in the light of new experiences. But they are there to be used by anyone not blinded by dogma. Marx believed that man created God in his image and not the reverse. Every Christian I know thinks of God in human form. For that matter I have yet to see in any Church a non-human image of God.

In a world where millions are starving, where man's technology has outstripped his sociology, I am not prepared to quibble.

Some years ago, at a meeting in Glasgow, I was speaking to a gathering of Christians about Socialism and Communism. I was suggesting that they were the expression here on earth of the brotherhood of man.

An old lady approached me afterwards. She said: 'My son, you are divinely inspired.'

Slightly unnerved I could only reply: 'You think I am divinely inspired, and I think that – if I am inspired at all – it is by my love of humanity. But if the result is the same, the end product is the same, does it matter to you?' We agreed that it didn't.

And that, I am convinced, is the truly Christian and Communist approach.

In the New Testament, Christ gives his own yardstick for judgement . , .

Then shall the King say unto them on his right hand, Come, ye blessed of my Father, inherit the kingdom prepared for you from the foundation of the world.

For I was an hungred, and ye gave me meat; I was thirsty and ye gave me drink; I was a stranger and ye took me in; naked and ye clothed me; I was sick, and ye visited me; I was in prison and ye came unto me.

Then shall the righteous answer him, saying, Lord, when saw we thee an hungred and fed thee? Or thirsty and gave thee drink? When saw we thee a stranger, and took thee in? Or naked and clothed thee? Or when saw we thee sick, or in prison and came unto thee?

And the King shall answer and say unto them, Verily I say unto you, inasmuch as ye have done it unto one of the least of my brethren, ye have done it unto me.

Then shall he say also unto them on his left hand, depart from me ye cursed into everlasting fire prepared for the devil and his angels. For I was an hungred and ye gave me no meat; I was thirsty and ye gave me no drink: I was a stranger and ye took me not in: naked, and ye clothed me not: sick, and in prison, and ye visited me not.

Then shall they also answer him, saying, Lord, when saw we thee an hungred, or athirst, or a stranger, or naked, or sick, or in prison and did not minister unto thee? Then he shall answer them saying, Verily I say unto you. Inasmuch as ye did it not to one of the least of these, ye did it not unto me.

The message is unmistakable. It does not mention which particular church you attend on a Sunday. It does not even enquire whether you go. It says quite simply that people should be judged by their treatment of their fellow humans.

Expressed in a social sense it means that you cannot be a Christian and do nothing and care less about the poor, the underprivileged, the hungry, the oppressed.

Christ opposed materialism and the materialists who worshipped Mammon. Yet the moneychangers are still with us. In fact they run this country. We call them asset-strippers, speculators, entrepreneurs. Far from being reviled, they are very pillars of the establishment. In some cases, pillars of the churches. When pillars fall, the structures which are built on them also fall. I think Samson understood that.

We live in a truly historic century, when man will emerge from the darkness of class society into the dawn of the new society of Socialism. Beneath the surface of the turmoil of events in this world today the process is discernible. We are witnessing the death throes of capitalist society, and the birth pangs and growing pains of Socialism.

Communists, Christians, socialists and all people of goodwill should be allies in the struggle to speed the process.

THE CHALFONT INTERVIEW

Recorded September 1975.

The law has no eyes, the law has no hands; the law is nothing – nothing but a piece of paper printed by the King's printer, with the King's arms at the top – till public opinion breathes the breath of life into the dead letter.

Macaulay

CHALFONT: In the Communist manifesto, Marx and Engels said that there were a number of things which had to be achieved in a country before it was ready for Marxism or Socialism; things like a heavy graduated taxation, abolition of inheritance, nationalisation of industry ... To what extent do you think society in this country has already been conditioned for a Marxist system?

REID: First of all I don't think Marxism is a dogma ... if it is then I want nothing to do with it. And *The Communist Manifesto* was written in 1848 – there's a lot of water passed under the bridge since then. That's the first point.

Secondly I think that for example the graduated tax system in this country ... to take that at its face value would be absolutely absurd. I am well aware that one of the growth industries in Britain has been tax evasion. This idea that the rich have been taxed out of existence is nonsense, patent nonsense. Similarly with estate duty ... there are ways round it, and they have the finest legal and accountancy brains working for their interests and, quite frankly, nullifying the effect of this legislation.

I think the cardinal point about whether a country is moving towards Socialism really is – are the wealth-producing resources of the country privately-owned and utilised for private profit, or are they socially-owned and utilised for social need. Given that yardstick I don't think we have made significant progress towards a socialist Britain.

This is my contention, but presumably people could follow up by asking about the industries which have been nationalised. I think they are basically industries necessary for servicing private capital, and our nationalisation has basically been capitalist nationalisation. We've nationalised service industries, pumped in public money and provided services for the profitability of the private sector.

I don't really consider this as an instrument towards a Socialist Britain.

CHALFONT: Well what would you say is now necessary to move Britain forward to the kind of society that you want to see?

REID: Quite frankly, the first prerequisite is that the people should consciously desire that change. In Britain the people have won, through struggle, democratic rights and they're precious. Therefore the first prerequisite is that the people consciously desire the transformation in this society from Capitalism to Socialism. Any other concept is elitist, and you can have elitists of the Right – and elitists of the Left – who want to impose solutions. They're really quite arrogant.

So first you must win a majority of the people for the concept of the transition of Britain from Capitalism to Socialism. I think secondly, assuming we reach that stage, you should aim to do it without civil war, and without violence, with the will of the people manifesting itself.

You first take into public ownership – I don't like the term nationalisation now, nationalisation has become a dirty word and I think public ownership is an area for experimentation and creative thought – you take into public ownership these institutions which really control this economy. Here I'm talking about the handful of big banks, the handful of big industrial companies and insurance companies, probably a hundred or so firms.

Take these industries, and these institutions, into public ownership, so that we can start to plan our society in Britain for social need and not private greed.

I'm not talking about the nationalisation of small farmers, or small shopkeepers, or owner occupiers and all this nonsense that you sometimes read about in the right-wing press. No, we're really talking about what Aneurin Bevan I think called 'the commanding heights of the economy'.

That's really what requires to be taken into social ownership. I could just make this point . . . I don't think we can talk about any extension of democracy in Britain, unless it takes the rights of decision making of the people into the economic field. As it stands we make great play of democracy and the rule of the people, for the people, by the people, etc., etc., etc. . . . What about economic decision making by the people for the people? It's the next area, the next stage in the real extension of democracy in this country, and without it I don't think we have got what we're entitled to call a truly democratic society.

CHALFONT: Well one of the things which comes out of that is the very obvious fact that you have not succeeded in convincing more than a tiny minority in this country that this is an ideal, or a desirable form of society. No Communist has got a seat in parliament, no Communist candidate in an election has yet failed to lose his deposit. How do you think you're going to do this?

REID: I didn't lose my deposit in the election of last year. But that doesn't really prove anything. Except perhaps a certain point you're trying to make about the electoral failures of the Communist Party. And that is a fact. But this is where we have to get certain concepts clear. I don't ever see a Socialist Britain coming about on the basis of a Communist majority in Parliament. And if you measure the feeling for Socialism by that yardstick, then you're tremendously under-estimating the position.

As I see it, the real dynamic force for progressive social and political change in Britain is in the trade unions, where there is a broad united left that agree – Labour Party people, Communist, non-party: if you want – militants. They are a force. And the Labour Party itself ... there are considerably genuine socialist elements in the British Labour Party.

If you want to talk about Marxists, it was Marx and Engels and particularly Lenin who recognised the uniqueness of the British Labour Party. It is different from all other Social Democratic parties in the world. It was founded by the organised working class, unlike the Social Democratic parties of Germany and France and the other continental, classical type of Social Democratic parties.

That gives a uniqueness to the Labour Party in the sense that developments for socialist change among the big battalions of the working class – and wider sections of the population – will at some stage manifest themselves in the superstructure of that organised working class which is the British Labour Party.

And I can only conceive of a socialist government in this country being a majority Labour government committed to fundamental socialist change, which none of the Labour governments even up to and including the one which exists today has been committed to.

CHALFONT: Are you saying that in the Labour party, and that includes of course the Parliamentary Labour Party ... there are a great number of people whose aims are identical with those of the Communist Party?

REID: Yes. But you see that could be then used and interpreted as a smear on those people. To the extent that there are people in the Labour Party – I maybe don't agree with every analysis they make, with every point – but despite that I recognise them as genuine socialists.

Now there's nothing wrong with that, because the Labour Party is supposed to be a socialist party. Clause Four spells out as its programmatic aim, socialism; and therefore, to the extent that they are genuine socialists, to that extent they are fulfilling the purpose for which the Labour Party was founded, which was not to manage British capitalism, but to end it, and to introduce Socialism in Britain.

Now I think that the people who really should not be in the Labour Party are those who are members of the Labour Party and who – despite its socialist objective – are quite clearly, philosophically, spiritually, ideologically and in every other sense like any group of Conservative front-benchers.

CHALFONT: Like a number of communists, you sometimes seem to use the terms Communism and Socialism completely interchangeably. When you say that there are a number of people in the Labour Party whose aims are truly socialist, how is that any different from saying that their aims are truly communist?

REID: Quite frankly, as I understand it, the concept of Communism is that once having achieved a socialist society, then economic and cultural and spiritual changes take place which lead on to a higher form of Socialism, based on 'from each according to his ability, to each according to his needs'.

To my way of thinking that's an historical objective which can't be precisely defined. It would be arrogant to try to do that. And so the real essence of the political struggle during our lifetime and beyond it, will be the fight for Socialism. I am very happy with that as an objective. It is the only one which I find tenable or realisable, and therefore I'm a socialist.

CHALFONT: By that definition you would say that the whole of the Left in this country including the Left of the Labour Party, the Communist Party, the far Left and the industrial wing of the Labour movement are all moving towards that kind of Socialism?

REID: We're moving towards Socialism. I say that once having had Socialism, or once having achieved Socialism, the world can't stand still; human society can't stand still. Therefore there will be a development from Socialism to some other kind of society. I say it will be a higher form of Socialism which philosophically we can refer to as Communism at this time – but to me it's almost academic.

In the whole historical period that we're viewing, the

essence of any progressive political struggle is for Socialism in Britain. And for that matter a socialist world.

CHALFONT: But where this matter is not academic ... in Eastern Europe and the Soviet Union to give an example ... the move towards Socialism or Communism has been accompanied by the most obvious deprivation of freedom, and, in most cases, an obvious police state. How do you think you are going to avoid this in your move towards Socialism in this country?

REID: Well let's get this clear. I'm not going into a large discourse on the deficiences of the socialist countries as we see them here from Britain. I think that Socialism inevitably develops in each country in accordance with the history, and the traditions, and many other factors which apply to that country, at the given moment of time when they carry through their socialist transition. We are, to some extent, all prisoners of our own history. We can break out of the bars that history has imposed on us, but we are all products of our own nation, of our own peoples, of our own traditions, of our own past struggles. That will leave its imprint in the form of Socialism, as applied in every country.

We have to watch that we don't get arrogant.

There is a thesis held in Britain that if the emergent nations in Africa don't precisely duplicate the Westminster form of government, then they can't be democratic. Now I do think we have to watch where we're going here. This could be arrogant. The British parliamentary system has emerged – and to some degree uniquely emerged – from the specific history and tradition of the British people.

Let me give you one example from contemporary history of a genuine socialist government that emerged from an election – from more than one election – and that is in Chile. Now that socialist government emerging from a democratic process, involved, in its socialist policies, a high degree of democratic rights for the Chilean people. There wasn't a political prisoner under the socialist government in Chile which included Communists. There wasn't one political prisoner ... there wasn't one political party banned, including the parties of the right. There wasn't a newspaper banned, there were no journalists in jail.

Then we had the coup, the junta, the re-establishment of Capitalist policies. The jails are packed with political prisoners, political parties are banned, newspapers are banned, journalists are in jail and being tortured.

Now I would say to you, that that's worthy of thought. That as Socialism emerges from a democratic process, that lays its stamp on the socialist government and state which emerges. When socialist government emerges from an almost complete denial of democratic rights, *that* must put a stamp on the type of government that emerges.

Now I'm not making some argument that would justify the recognition – or the lack of recognition – that dissent is necessary in socialist countries. I happen to believe that dissent is not a luxury – it's a necessity in any society which wants to be creative and grow.

And I do think, that in a number of Socialist countries, there has been a failure to handle dissent. And when I say handle I don't mean handle in a Machiavellian way, I mean even encourage dissent, because maybe from dissent you're only getting ten per cent which is pure nugget – wonderful stuff – but it's worth it for that, because that's the creative power-house of ideas. You don't get any progress in human thought when everyone is in agreement. I think unanimity is really a characteristic of the graveyard.

CHALFONT: I wouldn't disagree with that. Tell me though – to be more specific – when this socialist society, sometimes called the workers' paradise, is established in this country, what do you see as the advantages for the working people of Britain?

REID: British Socialism, I think, will develop along these lines ... this is my feeling. Already within a capitalist society we have fought for the social wage, the social services and so on. With varying degrees of success, for sometimes we had setbacks; there have been retreats.

I think that in a Socialist Britain, more and more the wealth of the country would go to the social wage. What I'm thinking of is free education, free health, free public transport. And why shouldn't organisations of the people have their holiday resorts, holiday centres? Kids could go away in the summer for four weeks free of charge. Cultural facilities – and I mean this in the widest sense of the world – could be virtually available to all, depending what their subjective tastes or appreciation might be.

And more and more your living standards, your real living standards, are determined by the social wage, and not by what vou have in your pocket at the end of the week or month.

You ask me the benefits of that. I tell you what I think they are.

It's not just an economic development, it's a cultural and almost moral development. It will end the rat race. It will end back-stabbing. It will be less important to get a few extra quid in your pocket, because, by and large, what you have in your pocket will be used for a very limited range of human activities and human needs. And one would hope that at a certain stage the social wage would take over almost completely.

And so we end the rat race. For the diabolical thing about a capitalist society is not the economic deprivation only of certain sections, but even the distortion of those at the top. Most of them have got there by crawling and back-stabbing.

What a way to live!

CHALFONT: That rat race has not been abolished in the Soviet Union, or in Eastern European countries. What makes you think you can achieve the Marxist economic system in this country, without the price that they have paid? Because the rat race goes on in the Soviet Union and the rat race goes on in Eastern Europe.

REID: I would part company with you here. I think that in the socialist countries they have taken fundamental steps towards Socialism by taking into social ownership the resources for the production of wealth. They are social, that's fundamental. Now if, superimposed on that, are elements of bureaucracy and elitism, it is not endemic in their economic and social structures. In fact it is contrary to the basis on which society is organised.

CHALFONT: You say that bureaucracy and oppression and deprivation of liberty is not an integral part of the socialist system. And yet it exists in virtually every communist state in the world today. What I'd like to specifically know, is why it can be avoided in a communist regime in this country?

REID: First of all I don't accept the statement that it exists or applies right across the card in socialist countries. For example it would be interesting for people to go to Hungary, to see the new ideas, the creative thoughts that are encouraged, the independence of views expressed. It's important I think to recognise that.

But more to the point, if you are talking about bureaucracy and pockets of elitist groupings appearing, it's my contention that in the socialist countries – and note I always say socialist countries, for they are not communist countries – in the socialist countries, they have tackled the fundamental question of economic power, all the wealth-producing resources are socially owned.

Now if, in such a society, you have got bureaucracy – which is an arbitrary taking of decisions and applying them administratively instead of winning conviction for whatever you believe is correct from the broad mass of the people – if that exists, it is a distortion of Socialism.

But in capitalist countries, bureaucracy – arbitrary decision making in the interests of a handful of people – is in the very nature of the system. Elitism, in the sense that in this world today we have – almost cheek by jowl – millions dying of starvation, and Paul Getty who has so much money he doesn't even know how much, that is actually a product of the system ... a logical product. And therefore to that extent economic deprivation, to that extent oppression, to that extent bureaucracy, to that extent elitist concepts, are natural to, and endemic in the beast.

Therefore I do not think it is logical to equate manifestations of bureaucracy in socialist countries – which are a distortion of their bases and of the system of society under which they live – and the same features, more so, in capitalist countries, which are the natural outcome of the fundamental organisation of the society.

CHALFONT: But let me give you a more vivid example of the contrast between communist – or what you call socialist societies, and capitalist societies. The major difference seems to me to be the difference of the possibility of choice. In capitalist societies – whatever their evils – people can choose whom they marry, choose where they go, choose where they work, choose their form of government, choose the people who govern them, kick them out if they don't like them ... in most socialist or communist countries those freedoms do not exist.

If you take the Soviet Union for example: at this moment there is not freedom to emigrate, there is not freedom to immigrate, there is not freedom to marry whom you please, there is not freedom to move between cities and to work where you please. Now why should that be and how do you think you can avoid it in this country?

REID: Firstly on the question of not being free to marry the person of your choice – I've never heard of such prohibitions in the Soviet Union or in any socialist country.

But honestly, let me first go back to the implication that we have a great variety of choices available to us in this country. I'm not so sure that that's true. Superficially it's true. I can go to London and I'm free to stay at the Savoy. It's not a freedom that I can exercise because I don't have the cash to do it.

In relation to having the freedom to work in Britain where you want ... I'll put this the other way ... they say we have no direction of labour in Britain. You'll have to tell that to the Scots. Over the last forty or fifty years Scotland has been denuded of some of its best lifeblood in terms of young men and young women who, because the operation of Capitalism in Britain devastated the community in which they lived, had no access to employment, no availability of employment.

Scots loving their country, wanting to stay in their own community, have had to uproot themselves and have been directed – not by formal political decision making – but through their bellies! To uproot themselves and go down to Coventry, to the midlands or other parts of England, till some of them have become almost nomadic. I've travelled up from London on a train during a bank holiday that was full of lads going back to see their wives and families. They've had to go and look for jobs in the south.

All of these things are important, because it does not mean that the freedom of choice that you're talking about really does exist in a capitalist society, in Capitalist Britain.

I could go on, if I wanted to, about the nature of the freedoms that people talk about in this country – and I am the first to recognise that we've won freedoms (incidentally freedoms won in struggle, not given to us) . . . but we've won these things and I cherish them, I value them. But I say that there is a whole area of freedom which doesn't exist in Britain.

For instance how about free from the fear of unemployment? That's a fundamental freedom. What about free from the fear of poverty? Free from the fear of insecurity? Free to bring your children up in circumstances where, whatever talents they have will be developed to the full? What about these kind of freedoms? Fundamental freedoms. There are youngsters in Scotland today leaving school who can't get jobs; possibly won't get jobs for two or three years. They come out of school, and they've more or less been told by the capitalist society in Britain: 'You're unwanted.'

A demoralisation sets in, and in about four or five years' time, some of them become so demoralised they become anti-social.

The right-wingers in this country, who didn't voice any protest about the denial of a certain choice, the freedom of the right to work – they'll be saying: 'Flog them, birch them.'

I think people in England should start reading Shelley again. In his 'Masque of Anarchy' he starts to talk about freedom. And he says at that time there were certain freedoms for the peasant ... like having a meal on the table for his children.

I tell you one freedom I would end. I've got to say this – I would deny anyone the freedom to exploit a fellow human being.

I would end that, and in ending that so-called freedom, I'm opening up new freedoms to the great mass of the people.

CHALFONT: But now this right-wing that you talk about. Do you foresee that in your attempts, and the attempts of other members of your party, to achieve this socialist and eventually communist society; that you are going to meet resistance from those who don't believe in it? Even perhaps to the extent of the use of force?

REID: You'll meet resistance. Certainly there is obviously resistance. When people have a good thing, when they've got wealth and they've got privileges, they always try to translate it into a philosophy which says that they're living in the best of all possible worlds. Voltaire satirised the feudal aristocracy. *They* thought they were living in the best of all possible worlds. And I'm quite certain the people at the top of British society are convinced – really convinced – that this is the best of all possible worlds. They're sitting right at the top, mind you.

So yes you'll have resistance. Now if the democratic will of the majority of the people manifests itself in a socialist government in this country, then, in my opinion, people shall have a perfect right in an ideological sense to oppose that government; to argue against its policies, and for the plurality of parties.

But presumably, if people of the Right who are in a minority, seek to frustrate and obstruct the will of the people – let's say by violence – then they are acting illegally, and steps would have to be taken to deal with the fact that they are breaking the laws decided on by the majority.

CHALFONT: What steps?

REID: The normal judicial steps. Let me put it this way. I am opposed to a Conservative government. I'll oppose it. I'll fight against it ideologically. But if I start to practise violence against a Conservative government, then I am entitled to be tried and to be punished. Because you can't say that I can violently oppose a government which has emerged from having received the support of the majority of the people. You can't run a society on that basis.

CHALFONT: How are you sure that, if it becomes necessary to deal with a counter-revolution of the kind that we've been talking about – if, for example, the right-wing of the political spectrum which at the present moment controls the forces of law and order, resisted the emergence of a Marxist regime – how are you so sure that you could prevent that happening?

REID: Let's take the Marxist regime ... that's language almost calculated to upset upper-middle-class ladies. It's an emotive term. Let's say a socialist government, elected by the majority of the British people, is meeting opposition – violent opposition – from the minority whose ideas and policies were defeated at the election. That government, in the interest of democracy, would have to take whatever steps were necessary – including force – to deal with the anti-democrats, who are repudiating the democratic will of the people.

Now if somebody tried to organise a revolution in this country – when they've got access to the ballot box, when they can seek to win a majority through the ballot box – if they, a minority, raised the barricades, what do you think the British capitalist state would do? It would say: 'You're not on. You can't do this. And if you don't pack up and go home, then we will bring in whatever force is necessary.'

CHALFONT: I think we may be confusing people. A lot of people think we *have* a socialist government elected in this country just now.

REID: Two factors. First we haven't got a socialist government. They are repeating the mistakes of previous Labour governments which will inevitably result, if it goes on, in their electoral defeat and the return of the Tories. They are trying to manage capitalism and not effectively to change it.

Point number two is that our electoral system is such in this country, that it's been a long, long time since we've had a government which has won a majority of votes at the poll. The present government did not receive a majority.

CHALFONT: How would you change the electoral system to avoid this?

REID: Proportional representation. I don't think there's any democratic argument against it. It's inconceivable that you should have a government that's only polled a minority of the votes, and sometimes quite a small minority. It really is ridiculous. Our system may have many merits, but it's a fundamental denial of our democratic rights.

CHALFONT: Now I want to go back to this point about counter-revolution, and the resistance to what you call a socialist government in this country. I want to put the point even more bluntly. Suppose the right-wing still controlled the army and the police, what would you do then?

REID: Quite frankly, you would appeal to the armed forces – as a government – to remain loyal to the country, to the nation and to its people. The tradition in Britain has been that the Army – and Army leaders are secondary – are loyal to the democratically elected leaders of the people. End that – forget about Socialism for the moment – end that, and you then bring in its wake real reaction, real brutality . . . bloodbaths.

The very fact that right-wingers can talk in these terms – and I know that the extreme right are talking in these extreme terms – is an indication of the fact that they haven't got a shred of democratic feeling in their bodies. They're for democracy when democracy expresses itself in the return of a Mr Heath, or a Mrs Thatcher. But whenever democracy results in the return of a government with which they don't agree, what they are basically saying is: 'to hell with democracy'.

In these circumstances, the socialist government would be fighting to defend the democratic rights of the British people. And if that ever came, then I would suggest that the next logical step would be to pension off all the Army officers who were the products of a certain social structure, and who were not prepared to accept the democratic mandate of the people.

CHALFONT: Who would take their place?

REID: Presumably Army officers loyal to the people, and loyal to the democratic will of the British people. Now that seems to me to be a fundamental with which all democrats should agree, no matter what their political ideals or outlook may be.

CHALFONT: Do you think the same should apply if a Marxist or socialist or communist government were to come to power by means other than an electoral majority?

REID: A socialist government should only be in power as a result of the expressed wishes of the majority. In Britain through an election, undoubtedly through an election. Where the democratic and electoral road to Socialism is open to you, you must take that road. That is your moral duty. Any other road is lunacy anyway, and any other road is an arrogant elitist concept.

You must have the will of the people with you otherwise you have no right to govern; you have no right to be in government; you have no right to be in any position to exercise authority. Unless it is with the permission of the majority of the people.

CHALFONT: Could you express that in slightly more concrete terms? So long as the will of the people in this country, through the present electoral system, rejects the ideas of Communism – you are prepared to accept that decision?

REID: Yes. Not only prepared to accept it, but as a sensible human being, to have no other alternative. I refuse to accept that any group has any right to do anything in terms of the political running of a country without the assent of a majority of the people. If you don't accept that principle, then you are outlandish, you are a Neanderthal man.

CHALFONT: You would go as far then as to reject the programmes of such organisations as the International Marxist Group, the Workers Revolutionary Party and the International Socialists?

REID: Oh yes. I do reject them. My main criticism is that they are really elitist in a sense.

If you cannot get a majority of the people through the ballot box, when it is available to you, then by what logic do you think you'll get a majority of the people to man barricades and sacrifice their lives?

If they are not going to vote for you, then they are not going to die for the ideas which they rejected at the poll.

SPORT, LEISURE AND CULTURE

What is this life, if full of care,
We have no time to stand and stare.

William Henry Davies

Culture is a much used word. What does it mean? Sometimes it seems to me a very narrow and restrictive word . . . referring only to a limited area of human activity. With relevance only to the production of an art form.

But there is something basically wrong with that concept. For man has an outstanding capacity to make virtually any activity beautiful and aesthetically pleasing.

To watch a good craftsman at work is a cultural experience. To see a footballer like Pele manipulating and controlling a piece of inflated leather with skill and artistry . . . that's culture.

When you think about it perhaps the best definition of culture is that of the anthropologist who describes a whole civilisation in the totality of its human activities as a culture. I should like to see this concept of culture both widely accepted and widely applied.

Historically it was necessary to have a division of labour in society. In order that the human species survived, it was necessary to work and to struggle and to grapple over long hours each day, each week and each month of each year.

And at that time there was an understandable division of labour between the hewers of wood and the drawers of water, and those who studied parchments and recorded facts of human knowledge, and those perhaps who went on to write poetry and experiment with language. To some extent I can still understand that division today.

But we must realise that man is now on the threshold of a world where this need for the division of labour will disappear. For in a truly socialist world, the time that man requires to spend securing the basic needs of his life will diminish. And as it diminishes, and leisure time is expanded, then an entirely different approach to education must be devised.

Such an approach will educate ourselves and our young not for work but for life ... for the enjoyment and appreciation of life to the full. It's in that context that I think we can see this correct definition of culture ... where people will work perhaps for a few hours a day, or even a few hours a week. Where they will work because they feel obliged to do so, not because they are driven to it. Because it is their contribution to maintaining the basic material needs of life.

But in addition to that we will be liberated in that we shall be able to apply and utilise whatever other talents we have in the fields of music and literature, of drama, sport and the whole spectrum of human activity.

And common to all human activity, particularly to that sphere we call artistic, is the need for man to communicate. He wants to communicate. He sees a relative truth in nature, in life, and does not want to keep that truth to himself. The real creative instinct is the desire to communicate what you learn from life to your fellows. (How spurious then is this shibboleth of art for art's sake. Art is not an end in itself, it is a means of communicating beautiful thoughts and profound understanding.)

Any appreciation of life in its infinite variety and potential involves aesthetics ... a word which in many instances should properly be used in the place of 'culture'.

And aesthetics are impossible to divorce from beauty. Beauty as created or expressed by man, rather than scenic beauty.

The means of conveying that beauty is art ... a part of our culture, though I prefer not to compartmentalise or categorise, since I think in terms of inter-related agencies acting from and upon human society.

The fulcrum of all activities is man. Man as an individual. And the subjective response of man to beauty is a well etablished truth.

It is a partial truth that beauty is in the eye of the beholder. For I may be stirred by the beauty of a piece of music ... a jazz interpretation or improvisation, while a sensitive, intelligent and close friend does not share that response. And this is true of other fields of music. Mozart, Schubert, Beethoven, can evoke a spiritual, almost ecstatic reaction in me while others react quite differently.

The same is true of the visual arts. I take pleasure in the clear cut lines of the Waterloo and Erskine Bridges ... others see them as concrete piles of a purely functional nature. One group tries to preserve London's St Pancras Station while to others it is a monstrosity.

And so with every art form. You can argue, as I may, about the appropriate response ... you may persuade others ... the dialogue may modify your own response.

But if beauty is purely a subjective response then there can be no basis for discussion, and there can be no social concept of aesthetics since for any dialogue certain criteria must be established. And if you argue that a work of art should impinge on the consciousness of others, then you begin to invoke common experiences. You cannot say 'I like it because I like it.' You are compelled to use words, an imagery that is essentially social. And thus you imply that not only are aesthetics subjective but also socially objective phenomena.

Aesthetics are no more static than is human society. The enthusiasm I had in my twenties for certain novels, some music and poetry waned later to be replaced by new enthusiasms. And the process of re-evaluation continues. Consider the revolutionary changes in art and music in this century alone. Did they come from within the artist?

I would say yes ... but is it co-incidental that they mirrored dramatic changes in man's knowledge, his productive capacity and the consequential social reactions?

For the artist also lives in the real world. No man is what he is, unaffected by society and the world into which he was born and in which he lives. Thus the artist's apparently subjective judgements on society, as expressed in his works, are largely shaped by his experiences in that society. And no artist can live in this rapidly changing world – a world with an innate capacity for destruction and despair, for construction, creativity and happiness without precedent – and remain unaffected.

Some try of course. The purveyors of trivia, possibly enjoying a temporary vogue. Perhaps they meet a need. Most of us need some escapism. There are times when a paperback containing material unbelievably irrelevant to the world as you know it can become therapeutic. The danger arises when such works become the staple 'intellectual' diet, for then society does face disaster.

We need the artist as we need medicine. For the role of the artist is truth and truth is beautiful. It need not be comfortable, for the truth rarely is. But it can never wear the ugly face of the untruth or of ignorance.

A great artist transcends objective difficulty. He or she explodes into the arena, and forces us to see ourselves differently. And while he may tell truths that are unpalatable, he conveys truths that are ageless.

The market in capitalist society says to an artist, 'You are free so long as your work is a commodity.' It says subtly, 'Conform or else.' But that cannot constrain him. He speaks the truth because he cannot do otherwise.

And socialist society should liberate artists with everybody else.

In the Soviet Union, this didn't happen. Artistic creativity was to be harnessed to the fulfilment of industrial and economic targets, short-term political objectives. Art was to decline into the role of propaganda.

But artistic or political conformity dries up the wells of creativity. And who then will tell society uncomfortable truths? For without truths you make mistakes and then repeat them. Whatever Soviet progress, it would have been greater if creative dissent had been encouraged.

A Shakespeare, Beethoven, Tolstoy, Picasso or Shostakovich cannot be muzzled by feudal patrons, the capitalist market or a bureaucratic committee. The minor artists are victims however and this is a tragedy. For although they tell minor truths, cumulatively they amount to a significant contribution to our knowledge, understanding and sensibilities.

We must learn from our own experiences and those of others.

A Socialist Britain must ensure the individual as well as the collective freedoms. This is neither a luxury nor a liberal concession ... it is a principle and the price of liberating the latent creative talent in our people.

This approach starts now.

Philistinism is the other side of the sectarian coin in the Left. 'Bloody artists, bloody intellectuals,' are judgements not unknown in the Labour movement. And I have known dedicated communist and socialist artists consumed by inferiority complexes because of this attitude. 'Learn from the workers,' they are told.

Some years ago a group of young communist painters invited me to look at an exhibition of their work. Afterwards they were anxious to hear my criticisms. MY CRITICISMS!

I can hardly distemper the bathroom.

The irony is that some workers of the Left consider artistic innovation with the deepest of suspicion. And in that their attitude is similar to the Conservative middle class. In music they demand 'the melody', in poetry 'the rhyme'. But the artist must pander neither to the prejudices of the proletariat nor to those of the petty bourgeoisie. To do so is to condescend, to treat with disdain. He must tell the truth as he sees it, and the rest is up to us, individually and collectively.

For the truth is harmful only to those who have a vested interest in oppression and exploitation. To the rest it is the light that allows escape from the dark, a light giving the perception to see the path ahead.

We should be starting now to prepare for that period when art will be no longer the property of some but the pride of all.

It dismays me how many people today respond to commercial exploitation of their leisure time. They are trapped by a social life outside their work which almost exclusively reduces them to the role of spectator, or participant in some form of mechanical and commercial manipulation such as bingo.

Part of the reason for this is that we have already established a certain leisure time without preparing people for the use of it. If some future archaeologist were to dig up the remains of contemporary Britain he might be prompted, in a lecture to the people of two thousand years hence, to explain that in the late twentieth century the dominant religion was known as 'bingo': 'There was a proliferation of bingo temples, and the civilisation seemed to be based on a crude arithmetical formula. The priest in his pulpit gave forth his incantations ... "clickety click 66", "Downing Street number 10", all the while imploring the congregation to keep bowed heads. Later a member of that congregation, apparently overcome by some form of religious ecstasy, would leap to his feet and shout "house". This seems to have had great theological implications.'

A caricature of course, a satire. But it serves to prove the point. I don't make this criticism in a condescending manner, for I watch my own mother use her leisure time this way, and I reflect that she left school at ten, worked hard for a lifetime to raise a family in difficult circumstances and now, in the twilight of her life, has been given a leisure which society has rendered her incapable of fully utilising and appreciating.

We must fight to continue this process of increasing leisure time for the people, but that being so we must also do the preparatory work which enables people to enjoy that leisure to the full.

The field of sport too must be reconsidered. We are often told that more money must be spent on sport because we want to do well in the Olympics ... because we want more winners of medals.

Others maintain that medals are unimportant and that money must be invested to allow people to enjoy more sporting facilities at whatever level of performance they are able to attain.

I certainly believe in the provision of facilities so that the broad mass of people may enjoy sport. For that is what it is really all about. And if the provision of these facilities does not produce the gold medals then no matter. It is still the correct policy to adopt. Yet although I have posed apparently conflicting alternatives, in fact mass participation, the provision of coaching facilities for all, will produce better performances among the top athletes. In this sense quantity will lead to improving the qualitative performance at all levels.

The lack of facilities in Britain is simply a scandal. And there is really no alternative to the spending of money, on more facilities, on more stadia, on more complexes such as exist at Meadowbank in Edinburgh with its provision for indoor and outdoor participation in many sports.

While saying that, we must also concede that there are many facilities already in existence in Britain which are grossly underutilised. Almost every town or city in this country has a football stadium used perhaps once a fortnight and occasionally for training. Arrangements could be made whereby the provision of local authority money allowed these grounds to be used for other activities.

This of course would require reciprocal co-operation from the clubs themselves. The clubs would have to become local sports clubs in addition to their footballing roles. But it would ensure that whole communities might benefit from multi-purpose participation in sports. And of course community participation would give an increased sense of identity with the club, from which they would also benefit.

Consider too the existing school facilities. Summertime in Britain sees the spectacle of children running aimlessly about the streets while the doors to the schools remain closed. Some of these schools have swimming pools, most have gymnasia, football parks, hockey pitches. All these facilities should be utilised all year, not only by children but by the public at large.

Once again I think we have too narrow a concept of sport. We don't think of it as embracing the real mass participation sports such as bowls, such as angling ... perhaps the major mass participation sport in Britain.

If we can extend opportunities in those fields and others like them, if we can re-examine our assets in respect of privately owned waters for instance, and exclusive fishing rights, we can encourage the right climate for widespread participation.

Whatever sport it is, if people are interested then there is a social responsibility, a responsibility at national and local government level, to make the necessary facilities available.

If we want our youngsters to participate, to want to emulate the performance of their heroes, then they must not have to travel from Glasgow to Blackpool to find the facilities for skating, or for swimming. Whatever the cost these facilities must be made available at community level.

For the more facilities we create for art, recreation and sport, for the creative use of leisure time, then the more economies we can make in the provision of places like Borstal.

REFLECTIONS, 1976

It was on a Monday morning early in February 1976 that I awoke after a restless, sleepless night, and wrote a letter of resignation to the Communist Party.

It had been a difficult decision to make, and not just for the obvious reasons.

It wasn't at all my being the victim of the 'God has failed' syndrome, for neither Communism nor the Communist Party had ever evoked a religious fervour in me.

In an historical context, political parties are transient. They represent social forces at a given time. And if these forces can represent, even in embryo, the future as well as the present, then they have a positive and constructive role to play.

For ultimately of course the future becomes the present, and the whole process means change. Social forces change, and in the changing can disappear as entities.

I can envisage a time when human society has evolved to the level where social forces with conflicting economic and class interests cease to exist, and in ceasing, make political parties both unnecessary and irrelevant. Not a one-party state, but a no-party society.

To view a political party with a religious fervour or commitment is a frightening prospect. To really believe in a God, in any God, requires a blinding faith.

It is unnecessary for such a believer to substantiate his or her faith with a catalogue of empirical evidence. God has revealed himself.

He is not subject to any known or unknown laws of nature. He is above and beyond such, transcending time and space. He is absolute and all mighty. He is the almighty God.

No person, religious or otherwise, should ascribe such powers and such qualities to any human institution. It is frightening when similar levels of adherence are applied to a political party, for it means political dogmatism. The party, whatever it is, must always be right even when the facts show it to be wrong.

When my resignation was published in the *Morning Star*, a close friend sharing many of my views said: 'I agree with you Jimmy, and I admire your courage, but I couldn't do it. It would be more difficult, more nerve-racking, more traumatic than when I left the Catholic church.' I find such an equation quite incomprehensible.

My own anguish, and that fairly describes the emotional intensity, was concerned with people ... my comrades, colleagues and friends within the Communist Party. Some of the finest people I know are British Communists. They are dedicated, self-sacrificing, non-dogmatic human beings. In terms of the effect of my resignation within the Party, they were my sole concern.

Of course there are others who would doubtless be pleased to hear the news. The 'closed brethren', as I think of them. Closed minds, and closed hearts. Mouthing out of context quotes from Marxist textbooks which they hadn't even read. A handy substitute for thought.

I lost no sleep over them.

I am still asked about the timing. Why February? Why indeed? But like everything else in life it was the culmination of a long process. The build-up had been gradual and imperceptible, even to myself. A reaction to a style of work, the challenging of the treatment of a comrade, condemnation of a sectarian approach. Apparently unrelated incidents which, over a period of time, began to coalesce into a general conscious critique within my mind.

Doubts, confirmed over and over again by experience, arose about the ability of the leadership to effect the changes necessary to open up the Party. To turn it outwards towards the people.

The concept of a democratic advance to Socialism, with all that entails, is not simply a matter of an insertion in a party programme. It required fundamental changes in approach, in the very structure and organisation of the Party, as compared to the thirties and forties.

Such changes did not take place.

I have no evidence in 1976, twenty-one years after the adoption of *The British Road to Socialism*, that such changes are even likely. Without such changes, the British Communist Party will not establish its democratic credentials to the British people. And this is the Party's Achilles' heel.

For many reasons, some false, but some based on experiences elsewhere, people still identify Communism with secret police, doors pounded in the middle of the night, and men hauled off to prison camps. It still conjures up a loss of independence, loss of personal freedoms, censorship and the banning of political parties.

You do not allay such fears by merely saying that 'we are different. Look it says so in our programme'. Or by protesting at the treatment of dissidents in other countries.

These things may be necessary but they are insufficient. For the often unspoken reproach is 'you say that now, but given power it will be a different story'. Or, in the words I heard addressed to one party candidate, 'if we put you in, can we ever get you out?'

To remove such distrust needs careful ideological explanation, but it needs more than that. For you win trust by deeds, by how you conduct yourself individually and collectively. An intolerant communist merely reinforces the suspicions already in people's minds.

After a television discussion Malcolm Muggeridge told the company that I was the only communist, and one of the few Lefts, that he would trust as a Prime Minister. His meaning was clear. He didn't agree with my views, but he felt that I would not abuse and misuse power. This compliment is much appreciated. It's unlikely to be tested in practice.

What is interesting is that although he is not in ideological agreement, he can accept my democratic credentials. There is disagreement, but not distrust.

I chose his example deliberately, since his views are currently so unpopular with the Left. But the story could be repeated many times with different communists' names and places.

So why the contradiction between trusting an individual and mistrusting the Party?

I must return again to a failure of leadership. Mistakes have been made, admit them.

Sackcloth and ashes need not be worn.

The Communist Party was wrong to oppose the war in 1939. The change to support with the Nazi invasion of the Soviet Union, has left its mark.

It was a complex situation. A government that included Chamberlain and his fellow appeasers could hardly be expected vigorously to prosecute the fight back against Hitler. Yet surely Pollitt and his supporters were correct in arguing for a support of the war, the replacement of Chamberlain by someone unsullied by the shame of the Munich betrayal, and a government of national unity pledged to an all-out war on fascism. Of course there were other facets, but the Communist Party was wrong.

Of course I can be accused of indulging in the luxury of hindsight, which, as every child knows, is an exact science. But what is infinitely worse is refusing to learn the lessons of history.

What we learn from the past is knowledge, for the future proves it to be true. Incidentally, when the war question has come up when I have been on a Communist Party platform, I have given the same answer. I have said the Party was wrong. The roof did not fall in. Nobody became hysterical. The audience appeared to appreciate frankness. All of which is not academic. For such points are embedded in peoples' minds, and in such circumstances the Party's defence mechanism starts to operate.

It doesn't really work. In dealing with past mistakes, honesty is always the best policy.

Fidelity to democratic principles has to be demonstrated, not merely proclaimed. In 1975 there was an incident which greatly worried me. The Communist Party worked and campaigned for a 'NO' vote in the Common Market referendum. I believe this to have been utterly correct, and that events will prove that it was so.

Nevertheless the verdict of the people was unquestionably a substantial majority in favour. To my horror an article then appeared in the *Morning Star* by a member of the Party's Political Committee urging communists and the Left to fight in their organisations and in the Trade Union Movement, for a boycott of the EEC institutions.

From my own experience, I knew this was not an individual expression of opinion, but the viewpoint of the Committee. This was confirmed when I was told that this was the Party line as expressed by a near-unanimous vote on the Committee. I bluntly refused to either accept or operate this line. It would appear that I wasn't alone. Party members and the Left refused to touch it.

How was this possible? It showed a divorcement from the realities of life in the Labour movement. Other issues arise.

If the leadership were prepared to ignore the democratic will of the people as expressed in a referendum, what guarantee is there that they will accept a democratic verdict on other issues? This is not to be confused with continued opposition aimed at persuading people to change their minds. A perfectly legitimate and democratic standpoint. But until a majority will it otherwise, the decision must stand. There is no other way of working.

In my view, Tony Benn, Peter Shore and others involved in the anti-market campaign, although bitterly disappointed, accepted the position with dignity.

The whole episode worried me, it had an air of unreality.

I had also been concerned over a long period about my experiences of Party rallies and meetings. *The British Road to*

Socialism, with its democratic radical socialist content, has apparently been forgotten. It had become something to be taken out and dusted down at Congress every two years. It wasn't references to the title I was interested in, but the spirit of the programme, and its application to the new stage of crisis in our country.

Something has gone wrong. I remember a poster produced by the Party nationally for one of the elections. It portrayed a tiny Edward Heath being squeezed in the massive fist of a worker. A fluid is dribbling from his trouser legs ... blood? urine? excreta? I was a candidate in that election and I blew my top. I tore up any that I could lay my hands on. As publicity the symbolism was in bad taste. Worse was that it was quite contrary to the *British Road*, and more appropriate to a wartime poster.

There has to be some rationale for these features to which I reacted. I can only advance the theory that the explanation lies in the politico–organisational structure of the party.

The organisational principles of the Party are based on what is called Democratic Centralism. There is nothing wrong with the concept ... it intended to combine democracy and centralism. I suppose most organisations subscribe to something similar in their constitutions without elevating it into a 'Holy Grail'. The application of the concept, how you interpret it and where you place the emphasis is another matter. Lenin was the main architect of Democratic Centralism. It was designed for a party operating in the Tsarist dictatorship of pre-revolutionary Russia, a country with little tradition of democratic institutions. The party was illegal, and had to work underground. Of necessity it was clandestine. In such circumstances, the emphasis on centralism was understandable.

For you could appreciate the difficulty of having a parliamentary debate on the timing of the invasion of Europe by the Allies during the last war. Or could you imagine a Paris conference of the Resistance Movement to discuss maximising their efforts against the Nazi occupation?

So in such situations one can understand the emphasis being

on centralised decisions with a limited democratic involvement. But as soon as the situation reverts to something approaching normality, then there must be a return to the democratic norms.

In the Communist Party of Great Britain, congresses take place every two years. But in practice there is an over-emphasis on decisions arrived at centrally which is both unnecessary and counter-productive. It results in attitudes and a style of work not really appropriate to the British tradition. For the role of the full-time officials is elevated to an unacceptable level.

Let me take an example from a few years ago. I was bitterly opposed to a certain party line, and expressed my criticism forcibly on the Executive Council. I also insisted on my right to oppose it in the Scottish Committee. But when I voiced my opposition in the committee, my right to do so was challenged. The challenge came not from other members of the Council but from others who argued that I was taking liberties with Democratic Centralism. In other words 'never mind the differences in viewpoints, just give us the party line'. There is something seriously wrong with this attitude, it is like Moses' unquestioning acceptance of the tablets from Mount Sinai.

The irony was that, having endorsed this 'party line', less than four weeks later – when the chickens came home to roost and reality permeated the armour dogma – the party leadership reversed their previous decision, and the same committee endorsed their action.

That was the last meeting of the Scottish Committee I ever attended.

The highest body apart from Congress in the CP is the National Executive Committee. It has forty-two members and meets every two months. In the last Executive Committee sixteen, or thirty-eight per cent, were full-time officials of the Party.

The only comparison I can draw is with the National Executive of the Labour Party which has thirty-one members, none of whom is a full-time official.

The Political Committee of the CP meets once a week. It has the responsibility for interpreting party policies between executives, and, when something develops in the political scene, to respond with new initiatives. It also plans and prepares the agenda and business of the NEC. This is not an organisational committee. Look at the terms of reference ... it is invested with tremendous authority. In practice it is the real seat of power in the Communist Party. The last Political Committee had fifteen members, of whom eleven were full-time officials.

Invariably, all reports of consequence are made to the Executive Committee by a member of the Political Committee. He outlines the analysis and proposals reached after long discussion by his committee. And on the executive, even when there is a full turn-out, only a few additional votes guarantee a majority for the proposals the PC suggests. That is the arithmetic of the situation.

There is an additional factor which I will call psychological. The National Executive is constitutionally the collective leadership of the party, yet a certain feeling pervades within it. A feeling which says in effect, 'The Political Committee must have given great thought to this matter. It comprises the leading full-time workers. Who am I to disagree?' A sort of 'they must know best' approach. In my years on the NEC I can remember not one occasion when the proposals of the PC were rejected.

On reflection that's an amazing statement. In the whole of history there has not been one group of human beings who have been continuously and consistently in the right. To be so is to be more than human.

When the EC gives its stamp of approval the matter then becomes party policy. Sometimes opposition to the 'policy' in a district or area committee is construed as disloyalty to the leadership, which in some minds is equated with the Party. Repeated expressions of disapproval or disagreement bring down the wrath. You are then disruptive, awkward, almost revisionist.

That is why I argued that *The British Road to Socialism* – a programme for democratic advance within the context of British circumstances – called for a re-think of the party structures. For to give the impression of a political monolith is to be at variance with the whole concept.

Some leaders of the Communist Party will characterise this as a slander. They will try to operate the defence mechanism. Yet I say to the members of the Party, this is an honest and constructive critique. It is no afterthought, as most of my friends know, and which can be proven. These views have been maturing over the years. I have expressed the same criticisms within the Communist Party.

Look at them objectively. You may not agree with all of them ... I may be partly wrong. Yet in total doesn't this critique have a ring of truth?

An analysis is neither proven nor disproven in a political party, but in life itself. In the actuality of our society.

Some communists may ask 'why state your views publicly? This can only bring joy to the enemies of the Left'. A seductive argument but a wrong one. I seem to recollect Lenin stating that there are not two truths, one for the Party and one for the people. The best guarantee that you are serious about wishing an open society is to be open yourself ... here and now. To think otherwise is to be secretive and clandestine when there is no earthly reason for so being.

If criticisms are constructive then heed them. The reactionaries' joy, if any, will be short-lived and far outweighed by the improvement in effectiveness of the Left.

I do not expect the leading officers of the Party to respond in this fashion. On all known form this doesn't appear possible. At the time of my resignation a spokesman for the leadership expressed surprise, as he claimed they knew of no serious differences.

This is difficult to accept.

Let the facts speak. I have not attended a congress of the Communist Party in Scotland since 1970. This was not a coincidence but a deliberate act of dissociation and known as such.

I resigned from the Scottish Committee at the end of 1972, and the letter is interesting in that it indicates that I wished to remove myself from an area of tension.

I declined to accept nomination for the National Executive in 1973. This provoked a long discussion with several leading members with the objective of persuading me to accept. Their arguments went thus: I was the best known Communist in Britain ... to refuse to serve on the leadership would be seen as having publicly disagreed with the party.

Eventually I agreed, but without conviction. And my decision was weighted heavily by two non-political factors.

First, I had just flown to London, having spoken at several public meetings, attended a tiring session of the EC and returned to King Street to have this meeting. I was really tired and all the indications were that the meeting would go on all night until I relented.

The second reason was personal and subjective. John Gollan was the General Secretary. Over the years I had formed a great respect and affection for this man. When it was implied that my refusal to stand might be interpreted as a lack of confidence in Johnny, I gave in. After the departure of Pollitt and Gallacher, he was the finest creative political brain in the leadership. Indeed I still believe that Gollan really wanted to make the changes which were, and are, long overdue. He was constrained by the very human quality or frailty of what I can only describe as shyness.

The timing of my decision to resign was triggered off by an issue that was not in itself of major political importance. However, you cannot detach one issue from what went before and what was likely to follow.

It was an industrial matter. A shameful decision was taken by a committee composed overwhelmingly of communists and Lefts. It's true that people make mistakes. But this was no mistake. It's also true that I could have raised it in the Party. This would have been worse than useless. With others I had repeatedly raised the unprincipled opportunism of the people concerned. We had warned that it could only result in the betrayal of workers. Our warnings were ignored and repudiated. These were good comrades, we were told. They sold sweep tickets and spoke deferentially to party officials. As a result workers were betrayed and some suffered. For me that was the last straw. Only the last.

There were other straws before that.

Basically I came to the conclusion that the changes needed in the Party would not materialise. People who were responsive to new ideas and new attitudes were voting with their feet and relinguishing responsibility. Their replacements were more in the bureaucratic mould.

Out of this kind of conclusion, other doubts arise. The thesis that there can be no advance to Socialism without a Communist Party is called into question. What if that Communist Party cannot emerge as a really meaningful, relevant force? Not emerge for a whole number of reasons including internal inertia? Is Socialism postponed indefinitely?

All thinking socialists reject the idea of a universal model applicable to every and all countries. It is possible that the indispensability of the CP applies in some countries, but not all.

Scientists since Einstein now acknowledge an area of informed and intelligent uncertainty. The future is not predetermined in every detail. To think so is obscurantist. What we can say is that within an area of probability this is most likely to happen, and then go out and work like hell to make a reality out of our probability.

On a broad canvas I assert as my belief that Socialism is the future for Britain, and for all countries.

How it will come about, what form it will take is uncertain.

For my part, I want to see it materialise without civil war and through democratic means. To make possible and keep open the option for fundamental social change with the assent of the people, concerns all democrats. This is why any shift towards an authoritarian government in Britain would be disastrous. For then change, even if willed by the majority, can only come about through violence.

The Left must be the custodian of progressive economic and political change. It must also be the watchdog of democracy.

In Britain the Left is potentially a massive force. But in what form it will emerge is still unclear to me. The conscious Left in the Labour and Trade Union movement must be the focal point of any realignment. That is where my roots have always been. I hope whatever develops, to play my part. It has always been so, and, in the nature of things – including my own character – could hardly be otherwise.